George W. Bush

MODERN WORLD LEADERS

Tony Blair
George W. Bush
Hugo Chávez
Pope Benedict XVI
Pope John Paul II
The Saudi Royal Family
Vladimir Putin

MODERN WORLD LEADERS

George W. Bush

Veda Boyd Jones

CHELSEA HOUSE
PUBLISHERS
An imprint of Infobase Publishing

George W. Bush

Copyright © 2007 by Infobase Publishing

Chelsea House
An imprint of Infobase Publishing
132 West 31st Street
New York, NY 10001

Library of Congress Cataloging-in-Publication Data

Jones, Veda Boyd.
  George W. Bush / Veda Boyd Jones.
    p. cm. — (Modern world leaders)
  Includes bibliographical references and index.
  ISBN 0-7910-9217-8
  1. Bush, George W. (George Walker), 1946—Juvenile literature. 2. Presidents—United States—Biography—Juvenile literature. I. Title. II. Series.
  E903.J66 2006
  973.931092—dc22   2006010609

Text design by Erik Lindstrom
Cover design by Takeshi Takahashi

Printed in the United States of America

Bang FOF 10 9 8 7 6 5 4 3 2 1

This book is printed on acid-free paper.

TABLE OF CONTENTS

ARTHUR M. SCHLESINGER, JR.

On Leadership

Leadership, it may be said, is really what makes the world go round. Love no doubt smoothes the passage; but love is a private transaction between consenting adults. Leadership is a public transaction with history. The idea of leadership affirms the capacity of individuals to move, inspire, and mobilize masses of people so that they act together in pursuit of an end. Sometimes leadership serves good purposes, sometimes bad; but whether the end is benign or evil, great leaders are those men and women who leave their personal stamp on history.

Now, the very concept of leadership implies the proposition that individuals can make a difference. This proposition has never been universally accepted. From classical times to the present day, eminent thinkers have regarded individuals as no more than the agents and pawns of larger forces, whether the gods and goddesses of the ancient world or, in the modern era, race, class, nation, the dialectic, the will of the people, the spirit of the times, history itself. Against such forces, the individual dwindles into insignificance.

So contends the thesis of historical determinism. Tolstoy's great novel *War and Peace* offers a famous statement of the case. Why, Tolstoy asked, did millions of men in the Napoleonic Wars, denying their human feelings and their common sense, move back and forth across Europe slaughtering their fellows? "The war," Tolstoy answered, "was bound to happen simply because it was bound to happen." All prior history determined it. As for leaders, they, Tolstoy said, "are but the labels that serve to give a name to an end and, like labels, they have the least possible connection with the event." The greater the leader, "the more conspicuous the inevitability and the predestination of every act he commits." The leader, said Tolstoy, is "the slave of history."

Determinism takes many forms. Marxism is the determinism of class. Nazism the determinism of race. But the idea of men and women as the slaves of history runs athwart the deepest human instincts. Rigid determinism abolishes the idea of human freedom—the assumption of free choice that underlies every move we make, every word we speak, every thought we think. It abolishes the idea of human responsibility, since it is manifestly unfair to reward or punish people for actions that are by definition beyond their control. No one can live consistently by any deterministic creed. The Marxist states prove this themselves by their extreme susceptibility to the cult of leadership.

More than that, history refutes the idea that individuals make no difference. In December 1931, a British politician crossing Fifth Avenue in New York City between 76th and 77th streets around 10:30 P.M. looked in the wrong direction and was knocked down by an automobile—a moment, he later recalled, of a man aghast, a world aglare: "I do not understand why I was not broken like an eggshell or squashed like a gooseberry." Fourteen months later an American politician, sitting in an open car in Miami, Florida, was fired on by an assassin; the man beside him was hit. Those who believe that individuals make no difference to history might well ponder whether the next two decades would have been the same had Mario Constasino's car killed Winston Churchill in 1931 and Giuseppe Zangara's bullet killed Franklin Roosevelt in 1933. Suppose, in addition, that Lenin had died of typhus in Siberia in 1895 and that Hitler had been killed on the western front in 1916. What would the twentieth century have looked like now?

For better or for worse, individuals do make a difference. "The notion that a people can run itself and its affairs anonymously," wrote the philosopher William James, "is now well known to be the silliest of absurdities. Mankind does nothing save through initiatives on the part of inventors, great or small, and imitation by the rest of us—these are the sole factors in human progress. Individuals of genius show the way, and set the patterns, which common people then adopt and follow."

Leadership, James suggests, means leadership in thought as well as in action. In the long run, leaders in thought may well make the greater difference to the world. "The ideas of economists and political philosophers, both when they are right and when they are wrong," wrote John Maynard Keynes, "are more powerful than is commonly understood. Indeed the world is ruled by little else. Practical men, who believe themselves to be quite exempt from any intellectual influences, are usually the slaves of some defunct economist. . . . The power of vested interests is vastly exaggerated compared with the gradual encroachment of ideas."

But, as Woodrow Wilson once said, "Those only are leaders of men, in the general eye, who lead in action. . . . It is at their hands that new thought gets its translation into the crude language of deeds." Leaders in thought often invent in solitude and obscurity, leaving to later generations the tasks of imitation. Leaders in action—the leaders portrayed in this series—have to be effective in their own time.

And they cannot be effective by themselves. They must act in response to the rhythms of their age. Their genius must be adapted, in a phrase from William James, "to the receptivities of the moment." Leaders are useless without followers. "There goes the mob," said the French politician, hearing a clamor in the streets. "I am their leader. I must follow them." Great leaders turn the inchoate emotions of the mob to purposes of their own. They seize on the opportunities of their time, the hopes, fears, frustrations, crises, potentialities. They succeed when events have prepared the way for them, when the community is awaiting to be aroused, when they can provide the clarifying and organizing ideas. Leadership completes the circuit between the individual and the mass and thereby alters history.

It may alter history for better or for worse. Leaders have been responsible for the most extravagant follies and most monstrous crimes that have beset suffering humanity. They have also been vital in such gains as humanity has made in individual freedom, religious and racial tolerance, social justice, and respect for human rights.

There is no sure way to tell in advance who is going to lead for good and who for evil. But a glance at the gallery of men and women in MODERN WORLD LEADERS suggests some useful tests.

One test is this: Do leaders lead by force or by persuasion? By command or by consent? Through most of history leadership was exercised by the divine right of authority. The duty of followers was to defer and to obey. "Theirs not to reason why/Theirs but to do and die." On occasion, as with the so-called enlightened despots of the eighteenth century in Europe, absolutist leadership was animated by humane purposes. More often, absolutism nourished the passion for domination, land, gold, and conquest and resulted in tyranny.

The great revolution of modern times has been the revolution of equality. "Perhaps no form of government," wrote the British historian James Bryce in his study of the United States, *The American Commonwealth*, "needs great leaders so much as democracy." The idea that all people should be equal in their legal condition has undermined the old structure of authority, hierarchy, and deference. The revolution of equality has had two contrary effects on the nature of leadership. For equality, as Alexis de Tocqueville pointed out in his great study *Democracy in America*, might mean equality in servitude as well as equality in freedom.

"I know of only two methods of establishing equality in the political world," Tocqueville wrote. "Rights must be given to every citizen, or none at all to anyone . . . save one, who is the master of all." There was no middle ground "between the sovereignty of all and the absolute power of one man." In his astonishing prediction of twentieth-century totalitarian dictatorship, Tocqueville explained how the revolution of equality could lead to the *Führerprinzip* and more terrible absolutism than the world had ever known.

But when rights are given to every citizen and the sovereignty of all is established, the problem of leadership takes a new form, becomes more exacting than ever before. It is easy to issue commands and enforce them by the rope and the stake, the concentration camp and the *gulag*. It is much harder to use argument and achievement to overcome opposition and win consent. The Founding Fathers of the United States understood the difficulty. They believed that history had given them the opportunity to decide, as Alexander Hamilton wrote in the first Federalist Paper, whether men are indeed capable of basing government on "reflection and choice, or whether they are forever destined to depend . . . on accident and force."

Government by reflection and choice called for a new style of leadership and a new quality of followership. It required leaders to be responsive to popular concerns, and it required followers to be active and informed participants in the process. Democracy does not eliminate emotion from politics; sometimes it fosters demagoguery; but it is confident that, as the greatest of democratic leaders put it, you cannot fool all of the people all of the time. It measures leadership by results and retires those who overreach or falter or fail.

It is true that in the long run despots are measured by results too. But they can postpone the day of judgment, sometimes indefinitely, and in the meantime they can do infinite harm. It is also true that democracy is no guarantee of virtue and intelligence in government, for the voice of the people is not necessarily the voice of God. But democracy, by assuring the right of opposition, offers built-in resistance to the evils inherent in absolutism. As the theologian Reinhold Niebuhr summed it up, "Man's capacity for justice makes democracy possible, but man's inclination to justice makes democracy necessary."

A second test for leadership is the end for which power is sought. When leaders have as their goal the supremacy of a master race or the promotion of totalitarian revolution or the acquisition and exploitation of colonies or the protection of greed and privilege or the preservation of personal power, it is likely that their leadership will do little to advance the cause of humanity. When their goal is the abolition of slavery, the liberation of women, the enlargement of opportunity for the poor and powerless, the extension of equal rights to racial minorities, the defense of the freedoms of expression and opposition, it is likely that their leadership will increase the sum of human liberty and welfare.

Leaders have done great harm to the world. They have also conferred great benefits. You will find both sorts in this series. Even "good" leaders must be regarded with a certain wariness. Leaders are not demigods; they put on their trousers one leg after another just like ordinary mortals. No leader is infallible, and every leader needs to be reminded of this at regular intervals. Irreverence irritates leaders but is their salvation. Unquestioning submission corrupts leaders and demeans followers. Making a cult of a leader is always a mistake. Fortunately hero worship generates its own antidote. "Every hero," said Emerson, "becomes a bore at last."

The single benefit the great leaders confer is to embolden the rest of us to live according to our own best selves, to be active, insistent, and resolute in affirming our own sense of things. For great leaders attest to the reality of human freedom against the supposed inevitabilities of history. And they attest to the wisdom and power that may lie within the most unlikely of us, which is why Abraham Lincoln remains the supreme example of great leadership. A great leader, said Emerson, exhibits new possibilities to all humanity. "We feed on genius. . . . Great men exist that there may be greater men."

Great leaders, in short, justify themselves by emancipating and empowering their followers. So humanity struggles to master its destiny, remembering with Alexis de Tocqueville: "It is true that around every man a fatal circle is traced beyond which he cannot pass; but within the wide verge of that circle he is powerful and free; as it is with man, so with communities." ●

1

A Nation at War

PRESIDENT GEORGE W. BUSH TUGGED HIS BASEBALL CAP LOWER OVER HIS face and slouched in his seat as the unmarked car with tinted windows left his ranch outside of Crawford, Texas. In the car with him were national security advisor Condoleezza Rice, also wearing a baseball cap, and Secret Service agents. The trip to the Waco airport took 45 minutes that early evening of November 26, 2003. Without a police-led motorcade, the vehicle became stuck in heavy Wednesday pre-Thanksgiving traffic.

The president was headed to war-torn Iraq, and the mission had to be top secret. Sharing Thanksgiving with U.S. troops stationed in Baghdad would bolster their morale in a war that was like no other war. The fighting in November was against insurgent guerrilla cells instead of against the organized army of the defeated dictator Saddam Hussein. It was next to impossible to say who was a suicide bomber and who was not.

But how did the president escape the surveillance that surrounds his every move to make such a secret trip? Of course, the fewer people who knew, the better.

Reporters and Secret Service agents stationed near the ranch didn't know he had left. An official White House spokesperson, who had not been informed of the trip, told reporters in a regular briefing that the president would enjoy a family Thanksgiving at the ranch and even gave out the menu. She announced that former president George H.W. Bush and his wife, Barbara, would be joining their son on Thursday for the holiday meal.

At the airport in Waco, the ground crew believed that Air Force One was flying off for routine maintenance. Earlier, a couple of print reporters and some photographers had been hustled onto the plane. They had been told about the trip just a few hours earlier and were ordered not to tell a soul or the trip would be called off. Absolute secrecy was necessary for the president to fly into Iraq.

Security was a top priority, not only for the president's safety but for members of the press as well. They were asked to remove the batteries from their cell phones so their positions could not be tracked. Window shades were pulled down to allow no light outside.

The door to the press area was closed while the president slipped on board. He wore jeans, a button-down shirt, boots, a baseball cap, and a work coat. Senior staff on board included Rice, chief of staff Andrew Card, White House communications director Dan Bartlett, and deputy chief of staff Joseph Hagin.

Mike Allen of the *Washington Post* served as pool reporter, which meant he would share his notes with journalists not on the trip. He and other press members joked about what the reactions would be from other reporters when they learned of the mission.

Richard Keil of Bloomberg News grinned and said, "The President of the United States is AWOL [absent without leave], and we're with him. The ultimate road trip."

The plane flew quickly to Andrews Air Force Base in Maryland and taxied into a huge hangar where the other 747 that doubles as Air Force One sat, fueled and awaiting the long trip across the Atlantic Ocean. Already aboard were six other journalists, who had stowed their cell phones, beepers, cameras, and other electronic equipment in manila envelopes, which were put in the cargo area of the huge plane.

President Bush walked across the white painted floor of the hangar and climbed the steps to the second plane. He turned back and saw the writers and photographers who had traveled with him from Texas. Because the terrific noise in the hangar drowned out words, he made the universal sign for a phone with his pinkie and thumb extended and held to his ear. He mouthed, "No calls, got it?" Making the cut sign to his throat, he again mouthed, "No calls!"

As soon as everyone was aboard, the engines fired and the plane took off. It flew without the usual running lights. The window shades remained closed.

President Bush slept during part of the ten-and-a-half-hour flight. About three hours away from Iraq and after communication with staff in the United States, he made the decision that the mission was officially a go. If news had leaked out, he would have canceled the mission at that point. A few days earlier, a German cargo plane had been hit by a missile. Even with its wing afire, it landed safely at the Baghdad airport, but that chance could not be taken with Air Force One. If Iraqi insurgents knew of the president's visit, they would attempt to assassinate him.

As the plane approached the airport, President Bush sat in the cockpit. Air Force One routinely makes steep, fast landings to minimize the time it is a target for a surface-to-air missile. This time, the pilot maneuvered a spiral landing, without benefit of landing lights.

President Bush rode a short distance in a van to the Bob Hope dining facility at the airport. Seated inside were 600

"I WAS JUST LOOKING FOR A WARM MEAL SOMEWHERE. THANKS FOR INVITING ME TO DINNER."

—George W. Bush

soldiers, members of the 1st Armored Division and the 82nd Airborne Division, awaiting Thanksgiving dinner. The guest speakers for the celebration were Lt. Gen. Ricardo Sanchez, commander of U.S. forces in Iraq, and L. Paul Bremer, the U.S. civilian administrator in Iraq.

The program started, and the newly arrived press photographers positioned themselves for good shots of the moment when the surprise guest appeared. At the podium, Bremer said the most senior member of the administration present was to read the president's Thanksgiving proclamation. Then he asked if there was anyone more senior around.

President Bush strode onstage. Stunned soldiers rose to their feet and cheered and whooped. Some climbed on chairs and tables to better see their commander in chief. Tears filled the president's eyes at the enormous reception.

"I was just looking for a warm meal somewhere," he joked. "Thanks for inviting me to dinner."

His message to the troops was thanks for honoring their oaths to defend the country. He said, "You are defeating the terrorists here in Iraq, so that we don't have to face them in our own country. You're defeating Saddam's henchmen, so that the people of Iraq can live in peace and freedom."

He congratulated the military men and women for doing a fantastic job and told them America stood behind them. He assured them the military would not leave until the insurgents were beaten.

"We did not charge hundreds of miles into the heart of Iraq, pay a bitter cost in casualties, defeat a brutal dictator and

President Bush boosts morale by surprising U.S. troops in Iraq on Thanksgiving Day, 2003. Instead of spending the holiday with his family, Bush made a top-secret trip to Baghdad and shared Thanksgiving dinner with American troops.

liberate 25 million people only to retreat before a band of thugs and assassins."

After his speech, the president worked the room, shaking hands with soldiers and taking his place briefly behind the food line to serve sweet potatoes and corn to the hungry soldiers.

He was soon whisked to a special room to meet with four members of Iraq's Governing Council, and in another meeting, he talked with Lt. Col. Sanchez and other military commanders.

After two-and-a-half hours on the ground, Air Force One revved up and took off, again without running lights. Not until the plane was out of Iraqi airspace and above 10,000 feet were the journalists allowed to file their stories. President Bush said he would not have gone without representatives of the press because the public has the right to know of the travels of the president. But he had been fully ready to turn the plane around if security had been threatened.

Back in the United States, George and Barbara Bush had arrived at the ranch to learn they would not be sharing Thanksgiving dinner with their son. Across America, while folks were preparing to watch the day's football games, they saw footage of the president celebrating the holiday with smiling troops in Iraq.

"It felt good," said Specialist Juan Deloera with the 1st Armored Division, echoing the thoughts of the troops. "It really boosted my morale."

"It helps a lot knowing that the commander-in-chief himself is going to come out here and make some of the same sacrifices away from his family, away from his home, to show that he is devoted and in the same position that we are," said Private Patrick McFarland, also with the 1st Armored Division.

President Bush told reporters on the long flight home that he'd thought of how lonely the troops would be over a holiday and he wanted them to know they were supported by the people back home. "Having seen the reaction of those troops, you know it was the right thing to do."

Democrats vying for their party's nomination for the 2004 presidential race were publicly supportive of the president's trip.

Senator John Kerry of Massachusetts said, "I thought it was terrific. I think it's the right thing for a president to do."

A U.S. soldier signals while on patrol in Iraq, in this photo from 2003. The invasion of Iraq has been one of many controversies for the Bush administration.

Senator Joe Lieberman of Connecticut said, "I don't have anything political or partisan to say about it. There are days when you have to say, we're not Republicans, we're not Democrats. We are Americans."

2

Growing up in Texas

GEORGE WALKER BUSH WAS BORN ON JULY 6, 1946, IN NEW HAVEN, Connecticut, to a family of high social status and a heritage of success in business and public service. Big things were expected of him. He had to live up to the family tradition, and he inherited some of the abilities that would allow him to do just that from several charismatic ancestors.

His great-grandfather Samuel P. Bush amassed a fortune through the railroad and steel industries, which started the family empire. As a businessman, he was well respected, and he was a charter member of the United States Chamber of Commerce. He also served as a key advisor to President Herbert Hoover, which began the family's association with high-powered political figures.

Prescott Bush, George W.'s grandfather, continued the family traditions and added success in sports to a long list of achievements. He played both football and baseball for

Yale University, enjoyed golf, and much later shot a record golf round in the U.S. Seniors Championship. Prescott Bush married Dorothy Walker, whose father cofounded Brown Brothers Harriman, the oldest private investment firm on Wall Street. The Walker family had several family homes, and among them was Walker's Point in Kennebunkport, Maine, which would be a place where George W. would play with his cousins and enjoy the close family ties of the Bush–Walker clan. The Kennebunkport compound is still a Bush family retreat today.

Prescott Bush served his country as a soldier in World War I and later as a U.S. senator from Connecticut. Whether at his office at his father-in-law's stockbroker firm in New York City, at his home in Greenwich, Connecticut, or at his vacation retreat in Kennebunkport, he liked preciseness and order. He demanded that his children be well-behaved and mannerly around him. His competitive wife expected their children to give their best to every activity in which they were involved and to be aggressive in sports.

GEORGE H.W. BUSH

George W.'s father, George Herbert Walker Bush, grew up in a home full of expectations, competitiveness, exquisite manners, and lots of love for family and extended family. George Bush attended a private prep school, Phillips Academy in Andover, Massachusetts, where he excelled both academically and athletically. Although he'd been accepted at Yale University, he decided to go directly from high school graduation exercises into the military. At the age of 18, he became the youngest pilot in the U.S. Navy at that time, and at age 20, in 1944, his plane was shot down in World War II's Pacific theater. He survived in a life raft until a submarine rescued him, although the two crewmen at the rear of the plane perished. Two months after this tragic incident, which had a profound impact on him, he returned to his ship. When his squadron returned home, he married Barbara Pierce and spent the remainder of his military service at various bases in the United States.

George W.'s mother, Barbara Pierce Bush, was the daughter of the president of McCall Publishing Company. She met George Bush at a dance when she was just 16 and was immediately attracted to him. They became secretly engaged the summer before he shipped out and before she started her freshman year at Smith College. She dropped out of college during her sophomore year when she married him. Once he was out of the service in 1945, they moved to New Haven, Connecticut, and George Bush enrolled at Yale in a special two-and-a-half-year degree program. The G.I. Bill paid his tuition, and his savings from his navy years paid the rent. Although his family was wealthy and willing to invest in worthwhile projects of family members, they felt a married son should support himself.

When George W. Bush was born, his father was a sophomore at Yale. As new parents, George and Barbara followed the parenting style of their parents. Barbara's father had told her, "The three most important things you can give your children are: the best education, a good example, and all the love in the world." She and George eagerly set out to follow that advice.

As the elder George attended classes, studied, and played on the Yale baseball team, Barbara took care of the baby in their small apartment where they shared a kitchen with two other families. She took little George to baseball games to watch his father play first base.

During George Bush's final year at Yale, he interviewed with several firms. His degree in economics would have helped him in a number of jobs, and he could easily have headed to Wall Street and followed in his father's footsteps as a stockbroker. However, he wanted to work with something tangible, not intangible numbers, and he and Barbara both wanted to make a life of their own, away from their parents' expectations. He accepted a job with an old family friend at Dresser Industries,

Proud father George H.W. Bush holds his son and future president George W. Bush in this 1947 photo. The younger Bush would spend his life following in his father's footsteps.

a holding company that had several oil-related subsidiaries, including one that made equipment for oil and gas businesses.

SETTING DOWN ROOTS IN TEXAS

George Bush loaded his brand-new red Studebaker, a graduation present from his parents, and headed for Odessa, Texas, a town where mostly blue-collar workers lived and worked. His job was manual labor—working on slippery rig clutches, painting oil rigs, sweeping the floor of the shop—but he gladly started at the bottom of the oil business to learn every element of it.

As soon as George found a place for his family to live, Barbara and little George flew to Texas. Their apartment consisted of two rooms; the Bushes shared a bathroom with occupants of the other apartment. By Christmas, the family had moved to another apartment, but because George W.'s father had only Sundays and one Saturday afternoon every three weeks off work, they couldn't make it back east for Christmas with the family. They missed their families, but they had wanted to make it on their own. Now it was time to create their own traditions in their adopted state.

West Texas, where every tree and flower had to be carefully cultivated, had nothing in common with lush green Connecticut, but young George W. loved the flat, dry, sandy place, which was his first memory of home. His father wrote to a friend about the two-year-old: "Whenever I come home he greets me and talks a blue streak, sentences disjointed of course but enthusiasm and spirit boundless. . . .The great thing is that he seems to be very happy wherever he is and he is very good about amusing himself in the small yard we have here."

Barbara Bush was also making the best of a different land-scape and a different type of social order than she was used to. As she later wrote in her memoirs, "You have two choices in life. You can like what you do, or you can dislike it. I have chosen to like it." Her positive attitude rubbed off on her son.

The Bushes had lived in Odessa for less than a year when George Bush was transferred to California. There the family moved around, living in motels and rented places, as George worked eight-hour days, seven days a week, assembling oil pumps and then selling oil drilling bits. While the family was living on the West Coast, Barbara gave birth to George W.'s sister Robin.

In the late spring of 1950, George Bush was transferred to Midland, Texas, 20 miles from their former home in Odessa. Midland was home to primarily white-collar workers, such as engineers, lawyers, doctors, and oil company presidents.

Many young couples from different parts of the country moved to the oil town, which had a population of 25,000. The

Bushes joined other families in the brand-new housing development nicknamed Easter Egg Row because the houses were painted bright colors and were basically the same floor plan or the reverse plan. The young people, mostly in their twenties, were optimistic in a town where fortunes rose and fell on wet or dry oil wells.

Things weren't as developed in Midland as they had been in the towns from where the transplanted folks came, but the new folks dug in and changed that. Leading the way were the Bushes. They worked on the Little League field so George W. would have a place to play ball; they raised money for the YMCA, where George W. could race his electric train; they headed committees for the community theater, where George W. could gain a little culture. They were also revitalizing the Republican Party in a Democratic state. The Bushes served on the United Way board, the church board, the cancer board, and any board that asked them. They were leaders in their community, and when it came to attending fund-raisers, they often dragged the children with them to swell the crowd. They introduced George W. to a world of socializing with a hidden agenda. By watching his parents interact with others on both social and business levels, he learned how to work a crowd.

The family loved Midland, George Bush wrote a friend. "We have had a fine year—we like Texas, the kids have been well. Robin is now walking around and Georgie has grown to be a near-man, talks dirty once in a while and occasionally swears, aged 4½. He lives in his cowboy clothes."

In the spring of 1951 and with financing from his uncle, George Bush started an oil business with a neighbor and worked even longer hours than before, but he still made time for his two children. Sometimes, he took George W. and his friend Randy Roden out to an oil field overnight to watch the drilling. It was an exciting time for the youngsters. The two boys would sleep in the back of the station wagon, waking up every couple hours to see if the strange night world of towers and lights and pipes had produced a gusher.

Life was good for George W. in Midland. He led the neighborhood children as they roamed from house to house, roughhoused with Robin, and played pickup baseball anytime he could. He walked or road his bike to Sam Houston Elementary School, and he was proud when his grandfather was elected to the Senate. Early in 1953, he got a little brother, John Ellis Bush, called Jeb because of his initials.

TRAGEDY STRIKES

And then one morning things changed drastically. Robin, age three, woke up and told her mom that she felt very tired and didn't feel like rushing around like George W.

Barbara took Robin straight to the doctor, and by afternoon the blood test diagnosis was in: Leukemia. The doctor thought Robin would live only a few weeks, but the Bushes took her to Memorial Sloan-Kettering Cancer Center in New York City for the latest treatments, and her life was lengthened by months. Barbara stayed with Robin. George Bush flew back and forth between New York and Texas, tending to his company's merger with another oil company. A nanny sent by their grandmother supervised George W. and Jeb. George W. was told that Robin was sick, but his parents chose not to tell him that Robin was dying. They feared he would tell Robin, and they also thought it was too heavy a burden for a six-year-old to carry.

Once during this time, Robin was brought back to Midland to visit, but George W. was told not to roughhouse with her. In the summer, the family went to Kennebunkport, and Robin was brought up there for a short while. But again, George W. could not play with Robin because she could develop internal bleeding with merely a touch.

One day in school that fall, George W. was carrying a phonograph back to the principal's office on a long outdoor walkway when he looked up and saw his parents' car. He thought he saw Robin in the backseat and was delighted she was back home. He set down the phonograph and dashed to the car. But Robin wasn't there, and his parents told him she had died.

Years later he wrote, "Those minutes remain the starkest memory of my childhood, a sharp pain in the midst of an otherwise happy blur."

How could a seven-year-old boy accept that his sister was gone forever? George W. grieved, and he talked about her. He'd learned at school that the earth rotated on its axis, and he wondered if sometimes Robin was standing on her head in her grave. He commented once at a football game with his father that he wished he were Robin. "Why?" his father asked. "I bet she can see the game better from up there than we can here."

George W. believed Robin was in heaven, but he felt a great sadness and he had nightmares. His father was traveling a great deal with his new merged firm, Zapata Petroleum Corporation, while Barbara Bush stayed at home with the two boys. Her grief overwhelmed her, and her hair started turning white. She did not understand how responsible her oldest son felt for her until, months after Robin's death, she overheard him tell a friend that he couldn't play because his mom needed him. That shook her. She dried her tears, hid her grief, and faced the day with a smile.

As time passed, the Bushes adapted to life without Robin. Another brother, Neil, was born, and the family moved to a big brick home with a swimming pool. The following year, George W. gained another brother, Marvin. But George W. was much older than his brothers, nearly seven years older than Jeb, so he didn't play with them much; instead he played with friends from school and from the neighborhood.

Baseball was always on George W.'s mind. He collected baseball cards, sending them off to be autographed by the players, then stacking them in a cardboard box and memorizing the stats of the ballplayers. He played catcher for the Little League team, and he dreamed of being a big league player someday.

At school, George W. was a leader, many times a spirited one, landing in his share of trouble. He once threw a football

Six-year-old George W. Bush poses with his grandmother, Dorothy Walker Bush, his father, and his beloved playmate, sister Robin.

through a window into the classroom when the class had been told not to go outside at lunch break. Another time, he was sent to the principal's office for drawing an ink mustache, sideburns, and goatee on his face. He was always funny, quick with a quip, and genuinely liked by his classmates.

By now his father was traveling more than ever with Zapata, leaving George W.'s mother in charge of the four boys. Her personality was a dominant force in her oldest son's life.

"My mother's always been a very outspoken person who vents very well—she'll just let it rip if she's got something on her mind. Once it's over, you know exactly where you stand and that's it," George W. said later. He could have been describing his own way of reacting to life around him.

Friends liked George W.'s forthright manner and sense of humor, and they elected him president of the seventh grade at San Jacinto Junior High. He played on the football team that year. Midland now had a population of 65,000, and George W. had made a place in it for himself by his friendly personality just as his parents had made a place for themselves by their civic work. But George Bush's successful oil company had grown an offshore drilling arm, and he needed to be in Houston by the Gulf of Mexico.

In the summer before the eighth grade, George W. and his brothers moved to a new house in the huge city of Houston and welcomed a new little sister, Dorothy, to the family. His parents enrolled George W. in Kincaid School, an exclusive private school. He quickly made friends, was elected a class officer, and played football and other sports.

In the spring of 1961, George W. returned from school one day to be greeted by his mother. She told him congratulations; he'd been accepted at Phillips Academy in Andover, Massachusetts, the same private prep school that his father had attended.

George W.'s childhood days in Texas were coming to an end as he prepared once again to move and make new friends, but this time in an environment very different from that of his beloved Texas.

3

A Different World

MOVING TO ANDOVER, MASSACHUSETTS, TO ATTEND PHILLIPS ACADEMY meant a major change in George W.'s life. Instead of the hot weather he was used to in Midland, with occasional sand storms thrown in, or the humidity of Houston from the bay, frigid temperatures and snow storms would be the norm.

But the weather was the least of his worries. At the age of 15, he was leaving a tight family unit to live with strangers. He knew only one person at his new school, his old friend Randy Roden from his Midland days.

An old school, Andover (as Phillips Academy is commonly called) was established during the Revolutionary War, and very little in the way of scheduling had changed from that time. Boys in the all-male school were required to start the day early with chapel or occasionally a school assembly. Classes started promptly with demerits handed out for a student being seconds late. By early afternoon, classes had ended, and two to three hours of sports and organized activities began, followed by more classes until 6:00. Evenings were for studying, and lights went out at 10:00. It was much more rigid than life at the Bush household.

Besides adapting to this highly structured world, George W. wanted desperately to live up to the reputation that his father had built during his years at Andover. George Bush had excelled in academics, in sports, and in student government. He'd been named Best All-Around Fellow, the highest honor.

Academically, George W. started off the year on the wrong foot. When assigned an essay on an emotional experience, he wrote about Robin's death and how deeply it had affected him. In revising his work, he saw that he had overused the word tears (in the sense of crying), so he pulled out the new thesaurus his mother had given him and found the word *lacerates*, not realizing it was a suggested synonym for the word *tears* (in the sense of ripping). His teacher gave him a zero and wrote, "Disgraceful. See me immediately." George W. pulled up his grade, and from that point on, he managed fine in a very competitive academic environment.

In sports, George W. was a junior varsity–caliber player in both baseball and basketball. At one tense basketball game, someone said, "Bush, get in there!" and George W. jumped up from his normal seat on the bench before laughter told him it was just a practical joke. By his final year, he was third-string varsity in baseball, but he warmed the bench more than he played.

In student government, George W. was elected representative-at-large to the Student Congress, but that was during his last year at the school, and he was never an officer. Still he was friendly, well liked, and knew most of the students by name, important characteristics for a budding politician.

Since he couldn't live up to his father's name, George W. decided to become a leader in a different category—frivolity. Other students thought of him as a funny guy, and he earned the nickname "Lip" because he was so quick with a funny quip.

An outgoing, social student at Andover preparatory school, Bush was a spirited member of the cheerleading squad. Although he wasn't a star athlete or student, he found an activity that made the most of his personality and his ability to connect with people.

He pushed the envelope where rules were concerned, daring the administrators to challenge his adherence to the coat and tie requirement. Sometimes he wore a T-shirt, a badly knotted tie, and an army surplus jacket to the dining hall.

Since he didn't excel in sports, George W. tackled cheerleading. By the end of his three-year stint at Andover, he was head cheerleader, directing school spirit. The yearbook showed pictures of the cheerleading squad crowding into a phone booth and straddling a tree limb with the cut line, "Bush and his gang. A heck of a lot of spirit from them."

George W. also decided to lift the annual spring stickball games to a higher level, crowned himself with a top hat, and called himself the high commissioner of stickball. The game, played with a broom handle and a tennis ball, was a great leveler of students. Even nonathletic types could play. At one game, a student who couldn't seem to master catching the ball closed his hands around a fly ball and made an out; George W., always a guy to reward a good deed, halted the game and led a standing ovation.

His friend Randy Roden recalled Bush's years at Andover for George W. biographer Bill Minutaglio:

> Being stickball commissioner revealed Bush's personality. He was a figurehead, well suited to deal with a diverse group. He bridged and brought them together. Bush was slightly impulsive, it was hard for him to bite his tongue and keep from saying something that would get him in trouble. It was a completely different heritage than his father's. His dad was from an oligarchic background. GWB was a prankster, mischievous.

During his summer breaks from Andover, George W. held jobs, courtesy of his father's friends. His first summer, George W. worked as a messenger and runner for a law firm in Houston. His second summer, he worked at the Quarter Circle XX Ranch in northern Arizona, building fences and anything else the foreman told him to do.

As the final summer drew close, George W.'s thoughts were more on where he would be accepted at college than on a summer job. He applied to Yale, following the legacy of his father and grandfather, and the University of Texas. He told his friends that he would like Texas, but as soon as he got his acceptance from Yale, he didn't mention the state university again.

The summer between Andover and Yale provided George W. another type of education—politics. George Bush had thrown his hat in the ring for a Senate seat, and he wanted his eldest son by his side as he crisscrossed the state.

In Texas campaigning style, George W. climbed on the Bush bandwagon with his mother and father; the Black Mountain

Boys, who opened each rally with country and western tunes; and the Bush Bluebonnet Belles, a female singing group. George W. told supporters that his father was better at what he was doing than those around him, and he believed wholeheartedly in his father's abilities. His father was his hero.

THE TRANSITION TO YALE

His ties with his father didn't make adjusting to Yale any easier. George W's father had again excelled in sports and academics there, had been president of his fraternity, and been tapped for the secret society Skull and Bones. George W. gave those areas the old college try. He was a mediocre pitcher on the freshman baseball team, but by his final year, he had managed to make the first team in rugby. In academics, he was again an average student, although he did much better in subjects he liked, and he credited his prep school with teaching him how to think and make it in a college environment. He majored in history, with emphasis on American and European history, to which he had been drawn at Andover through the efforts of an exceptional teacher, Tom Lyons. "He taught me that history brings the past and its lessons to life, and those lessons can often help predict the future," George W. later wrote in *A Charge to Keep*.

George W.'s transition from the rigid structure at Andover to the freer organization of college life included having lots of fun, and that included joining his father's fraternity, Delta Kappa Epsilon (DKE), and later becoming president of that social group. During the membership recruitment period called rush, a few potential members called pledges were asked to name the other pledges. Most pledges could name four or five others. When George W. was called on, his remarkable memory served him well, and he named all 54 people in the room.

The DKE house boasted the longest bar on campus, and George W.'s two brushes with the law directly involved alcohol. The first occurred one December when he and other DKEs, laughing and making a lot of noise, were driving around

STILL, GEORGE W. FOLLOWED HIS FATHER'S EXAMPLE OF BOUNCING BACK, ANALYZING THE EVENT, KNOWING HE GAVE IT HIS BEST SHOT, AND MOVING ON.

downtown. George W. spied a wreath on a storefront and thought it should decorate the DKE house. No sooner had he taken it than patrolling New Haven police arrested him and charged him with disorderly conduct. He later referred to it as the "Christmas wreath caper." The revelers apologized and the charges were dropped.

The second incident occurred at a Yale-Princeton football game at Princeton, with Yale victorious for the first time in eight years. George W., who had been drinking, and about 30 others raced onto the field to tear down the wooden goalpost. He was sitting on the crossbar when campus police grabbed him along with a handful of others, escorted them off the field, and told them to get out of town.

Although caught up in school life—classes, studying, and partying—George W. kept informed of his father's political activities. In November of his freshman year, he went home for election night and posted voting returns as they came in to the campaign's headquarters. It was not a pleasant job. His father was defeated for the office, and George W. felt as dejected as the others in his family. It did not help that the atmosphere at Yale was very liberal and George Bush's views were rather conservative; George W. took the talk he heard on campus as personal criticism of Bush family politics. Still, he followed his father's example of bouncing back, analyzing the event, knowing he gave it his best shot, and moving on.

George W. had the utmost respect for his father, but that didn't keep him from making some bad judgment calls that

While at Yale, Bush studied, belonged to a fraternity, and learned about politics as he followed his father's career.

reflected on his father. His summer job before his sophomore year was working on an inland Louisiana oil barge anchored in 20 feet of water. He worked seven to ten days on and then had seven to ten days off. During his off periods, he returned to Houston and partied with his friends. A week before his summer commitment was up, George W. told his fellow crew members that he wasn't coming back; he wanted to be with friends and his girlfriend in Houston. When he got back to the city, he was called to his father's office.

"You agreed to work a certain amount of time, and you didn't," his father told him. "I just want you to know that you have disappointed me."

George W. was crushed. Even though a few hours later his father asked him to accompany him to a Houston Astros game, so he obviously wasn't holding a grudge, George W. would always remember how it felt to let his father down.

He returned to Houston the following summer and worked as a sporting goods salesman at Sears. He devoted the break from school to seeing his girlfriend, Cathryn Wolfman, and helping with his father's new campaign for the United States Congress from Texas's Seventh District.

George W. returned to Houston from Yale in November for "Reality Day," the Bush term for Election Day. This time when he posted the voting results, there was reason for celebration, for whoops and yells. George Bush had been elected to Congress.

Before his father could assume his congressional seat in Washington, D.C., at the January swearing-in, George W. had made a big decision about his own life. He gave an engagement ring to Cathryn for Christmas. Although they did not set a wedding date, they planned to marry the summer before his senior year. They talked long-distance during the spring semester, postponed the wedding, but continued to see each other the following summer, while George W. worked as a bookkeeper for a securities firm. When no marriage plans had been made by his senior year, he figured the wedding was off, but their engagement wasn't officially ended for several more months.

Talk among Yale's 1968 graduating seniors, the last all-male class at Yale, centered on the war in Vietnam and their student draft deferments, which would expire the moment they graduated college. Some antiwar seniors talked of heading to Canada to avoid the draft; some enrolled in medical school; a few signed up for the military. Over Christmas break, George W. checked into pilot training in the Texas Air National Guard.

He wanted to return to Texas. He looked forward to getting away from what he called the intellectual snobs at school as soon as he graduated in June; he had never fit into the anti-establishment mood during those turbulent times. He wanted to go home to Texas.

CHAPTER
4
What Path to Take?

SOME FOLKS SAID THAT GEORGE W. HAD A FEW STRINGS PULLED TO GET into the Texas Air National Guard, where open slots were rare at that time. It was a fairly safe way of being in the military while avoiding active duty in Vietnam, where an unpopular war raged. Sons of influential people signed up to do their patriotic duty stateside in the Guard. Congressman George Bush denied that he asked anyone to help his son get a coveted spot. George W. said he wanted to be a pilot like his father, was accepted because he passed the pilot tests, and found an open slot because few men were willing to sign away the six years necessary for flight training and weekend duties. Later, a Bush family friend admitted, although he had not been asked to do it, that he made a call to the general in charge of the Guard informing him that Congressman Bush's son was trying to get into that branch of the military.

George W. spent basic training at Lackland Air Force Base in San Antonio in late July and August. Upon completion, he was to report to a base in Houston until his air force flight training began in November. A couple weeks after he finished basic training, he was granted leave to work on a political campaign in Florida until after Election Day in November, returning to Houston occasionally for weekend duty.

Working as an aide for the senatorial campaign of Congressman Edward J. Gurney of Florida, George W.'s job was to herd press corps members on and off the campaign plane and get them into hotel rooms. This taught him to handle difficult pressroom situations using his trademark humor and brazen straightforward manner of dealing with people.

Second Lieutenant George W. Bush analyzed the campaign, which was hard-fought and an uphill battle for the conservative Gurney. The politician focused on three issues. He hammered them over and over and was not detoured by side issues. He did not soften his position, and once he won the election, Gurney said that partisan politics were set aside now for the good of the people and that he'd work toward implementing his three issues. George W. noted how effective the focused approach worked. Gurney never wavered from his message, and by observing this politician, George W. learned how to wage a winning campaign.

Toward the end of November, George W. arrived at Moody Air Force Base in Valdosta, Georgia. Among some 70 pilot trainees, George W. was the only Guardsman; the others were regular military. George W. actually did very well in pilot school. His remarkable memory served him in good stead where charts and diagrams were involved. A few trainees felt George W. received preferential treatment from instructors who were after promotions and thought they might get recommendations from Congressman Bush.

But Norman Dotti, who trained with George W. said, "Everybody knew who he was and who his father was. They knew he was there from the Texas Air National Guard. If anybody felt negative about that, nobody said anything. He was certainly competent. He didn't put on airs."

Joe Chaney, an airman from Alabama, said, "We worked hard and played hard, throwing dice and talking about flying and drinking. We went to the bar, played bar games, swapped lies. He was extremely intelligent, very witty and humorous."

Midway thorough training, other pilot trainees watched as a government plane landed from Andrews Air Force Base, picked up George W., and flew him to Washington. President Nixon had ordered the plane because his daughter, Tricia, needed a dinner date. When he returned to his base, George W. refused to give details about the date except to say it wasn't very long. Other airmen were amazed that he could leave the base, when they were stuck in the summer heat of Georgia.

In December 1969, pilot training was over, and George W. and half his classmates earned their wings. He headed back to Houston for an assignment flying night maneuvers out of Ellington Air Force Base. Because he was a congressman's son, the Texas Air National Guard used George W. in one of its promotional ads, claiming he got his kicks from flying a jet.

FINDING HIS WAY

He also got his kicks from fun and was in the center of activity at the singles apartment complex where he lived. He drank beer with other tenants, played volleyball in one of the six swimming pools, and dated extensively. He lived in a cluttered apartment with clothes and cans on the floor and drove a cluttered car with clothes and papers on the seats, but he lived a fairly uncluttered life without lots of responsibilities.

A few months remained before George W. completed the two-year active duty phase of his training. His father was running for the Senate again, and this time George W. was an occasional member of the campaign team, flying off on one-day excursions. Wearing his National Guard flight jacket, he would step to the microphone and say a few words praising his father.

In June, George W. began his four-year inactive duty, which required that he fly the F-102 jet only a few times a month. At

George W. Bush climbs the steps of a Texas National Guard fighter plane in this photo. Prior to the 2004 presidential election, controversies arose regarding Bush's service record.

loose ends the rest of the time, he joined his father's campaign, traveling across the state with a busload of college interns and speaking on behalf of his father. He described his role as "surrogate candidate," since he addressed the many, many issues exactly as his conservative father would have if he were there. George W.'s own opinions were more moderate and less conservative.

George Bush lost the Senate race to Lloyd Bentsen, and George W. heard charges of carpetbagger because of his father's eastern roots and Ivy League education. George W. took the loss hard, even though his father was quickly appointed to the prestigious job of ambassador to the United Nations by President Nixon.

First Lieutenant George W. Bush now reported one weekend a month to the base, which allowed plenty of time for him to pursue a career, but he had no real direction, no goal, and no driving passion. He drifted along, visiting his parents in New York City and attending Mets games while there, courtesy of his great-uncle, who was part owner.

He applied to law school at the University of Texas but was turned down, and what he called his "nomadic period" began with a series of short-term jobs, obtained through his father's contacts. He signed on with Stratford of Texas, an agricultural development company, as a management trainee and learned to prepare reports, give presentations, and negotiate purchase agreements for horticultural operations in the United States and in Central America. After nine months on the job, he knew that was not the type of career he wanted and he resigned.

Between jobs again, he thought about running for a legislative position in the Texas House or Senate. The *Houston Post* ran a short article about George W. pondering the possibility. But after a talk with his father, who told him he didn't yet have the experience to run, he decided against the idea.

Instead, he followed his father's advice and took a job as political director on the senate campaign of Winton M. Blount

Winton Blount (speaking) was the U.S. Postmaster General from 1969 through 1971. George W. Bush served as the political director of Blount's 1972 campaign for Senate.

in Alabama. Here he could learn more of the ins and outs of campaigning and the issues facing those who choose government service as a career. He set up rallies, handed out literature, and met Republican workers in small towns. He watched the candidates give speeches and noted how Blount's opponent was much more personable with the public. Blount stayed on his message, hitting his main issues, but he didn't have the personality to converse with the voters on a personal level. It was no surprise to George W. that his candidate was beaten at the polls.

George W. was allowed to temporarily transfer to the 187th Tactical Reconnaissance Group in Montgomery, Alabama, while he worked on the campaign. After the election, he returned to flying out of his home base in Houston. Once again he was out of a full-time job.

His father was now serving as chairman of the Republican National Convention. On a Christmas trip to visit his parents in their home in Washington, D.C., George W. caroused with friends. One evening, he took his younger brother Marvin with him, and the two drank alcohol. Driving home, George W. hit a neighbor's trash can, which stuck to the wheel of his car. The banging noise continued until he parked in his parents' driveway. Once they were in the house and the family saw the state of 15-year-old Marvin, an angry George Bush called his oldest son into the den.

"I hear you're looking for me," said an inebriated George W. "You wanna go mano a mano right here?"

Jeb Bush stepped in to calm the situation between his brother and his father. To sound a positive note, he announced that George W. had been accepted at Harvard Business School. George Bush told his son he should seriously consider that, but George W. said he wasn't going. He had just wanted to see if he could get in.

FINDING STRUCTURE FOR HIS LIFE

His acceptance to Harvard was for the fall of 1973, nine months away. To fill the gap, he took yet another job that his father recommended. While still flying for the Guard, George W. began working for the Professional United Leadership League (PULL), an organization that linked famous athletes and celebrities with Houston's inner-city kids. George W. worked on fund-raising, public relations, and mentoring the children.

Senior counselor Muriel Simmons Henderson remembered him from that job: "He never put himself in the position of looking down his nose at someone, like 'I've got all this money, my father is George Bush.' He never talked about his father. He was so down to earth. You could not help liking him. He was always fun."

Kindergartner Jimmy Dean was special to George W. The boy hung on George W.'s every word and also hung on his leg or his arm, following him like a shadow. When the tough boy would show up without shoes or a shirt, George W. took him shopping. Much later, George W. learned that as a teen Jimmy was killed by gunfire.

In urban Houston, George W. saw a different element of life than the country club and private school set he was used to. He felt he made a difference in children's lives, and he liked helping them.

George W. requested an early discharge from the Texas Air National Guard so he could attend Harvard. His enlistment period was not up until May 1974, but he was given early release and transferred to a reserve unit in Boston. His military file said: "Lt. Bush's major strength is his ability to work with others. Lt. Bush is very active in civic affairs in the community and manifests a deep interest in the operation of our government."

He was also deeply interested in how business organizations worked. Harvard Business School taught through case studies of businesses, covering what went wrong and how to fix them. Reading a hundred to three hundred pages a day and writing a paper a week took time and energy, and George W. settled down to learn all he could.

Of course, George W. was not one to be all work and no play. He would not have been himself if he hadn't enjoyed the people around him. He befriended other students, played intramural baseball and softball, and drank at local bars, favoring a country-western bar that reminded him of Texas. In a time when there were lots of antiwar, anti-Nixon, antiestablishment feelings on campus, he proudly wore his National Guard flight jacket. In his yearbook picture, he wore a rumpled sports shirt, not a coat and tie. He didn't fit in, but it didn't bother him. He sat at the back of classrooms chewing tobacco and spitting into a cup, which didn't fit the mold of a student at Harvard Business School.

He was 27 and had been out of Yale for five years, but he settled into school to learn how to run a business. His mother believed Harvard gave him structure, something he sorely needed at that time in his life.

By the time he graduated from Harvard Business School, George W. had determined that the place to make a fortune was where he felt most at home, Midland, Texas. Another oil boom beckoned him to the place of his childhood. Before he started west, he detoured for a few weeks' vacation to China, where his father was now chief of the U.S. Liaison Office. George W. enjoyed the family and the sightseeing, but it was time for him to establish a life for himself.

Armed with around $15,000 seed money left over from his Bush–Walker education fund, he set his sights on Midland with the plan of learning the oil business. He was setting out on his own, but he was once again following in his father's footsteps.

5

The Family Business

AHH. . . . TEXAS! MIDLAND WAS ALL HE THOUGHT IT WOULD BE: HOT, DUSTY, and home. Several of George W.'s childhood friends had returned to Midland after starting careers in bigger cities, so he had a circle of friends from his first days back in West Texas, and he made new ones, too.

George W. quickly formed bonds with Don Evans, Charlie Younger, and Joe O'Neill, who would remain lifelong friends. George W. was known as a friendly guy, but he qualified exactly what a friend was. A friend was "someone who is loyal. An acquaintance is someone who might not be loyal. Loyal means that I'm with you when times are good or times are bad." Loyalty was number one in importance to his father, and George W. valued it just as much.

He turned his rented two-room guesthouse into a bachelor pad. With his typical housekeeping ways, the floors were soon covered with newspapers and clothes. His bed frame was held together with neckties, which he figured was a much better use for them than around his neck.

Many of his parents' old friends still lived in the oil town, and George W. turned to them for advice on starting his new life. Be a land man, they told him. Serving as the middleman between oil drillers and landowners was the place to start in the oil business, and it was a natural choice for a history major trained in research.

George W. went to the courthouse and looked up deeds. He found out who owned the surface of land, and he found out who owned the earth below. Land ownership was stratified. Farmers would sell off mineral rights to certain depths. One oil company could own down to approximately 5,000 feet. Another might own mineral rights from 5,001 to 8,000 feet, and another company could own the rights down another thousand feet.

Once he determined who owned land in the unmarked, unfenced dry Texas land and checked many handwritten deeds to see who owned oil and gas rights, it was time to knock on doors of farmhouses and talk to farmers about selling their mineral rights. George W. would firmly shake hands while looking the owner straight in the eyes. In good-ol'-boy fashion, he'd talk about the weather, discuss the local high school football team, and finally get around to talking about oil.

His job was actually linking together different types of people and persuading them that they wanted to connect in a business deal. As he had done in school, as stickball commissioner and fraternity president, he learned the needs of the men involved and initiated action. The land man job let him use the knowledge he'd gained at Harvard Business School and be his own boss.

"I wasn't about to do something that I didn't want to do. I was single. My overhead was extremely low. I knew I didn't want to work for anybody for a while," he later told a reporter for the *Dallas Morning News*.

Money he earned from working as a land man kept George W. financially solvent. He rationed out his seed money from the Walker–Bush fund and lived on a tight budget. He wore hand-me-down shirts from a friend, he drove a car that needed a paint job, and he used Scotch tape to repair his loafers. As a practical joke to point out his miserly ways, a friend took old Christmas cards from an oil company, crossed off the name, and forged George W. Bush's signature. People around Midland got a good laugh when they received the recycled Christmas cards.

George W. had fun with his friends, too. He jogged most mornings, and when he passed an old oilman on the track, he pulled down the man's running shorts and zipped right past him. He and Charlie Younger went to nearby Odessa, drank a little too much, and climbed onstage behind Willie Nelson and sang along. Once he decided to take Don Evans flying in a rented Cessna. George W. checked out the plane, climbed inside, and discovered he didn't know how to fly it. When he finally got it started, he lifted the nose straight up as he would a jet and nearly stalled the plane. He managed a wobbly landing. Then, as if the first attempt had never happened, he asked Don if he wanted to fly around Midland. This time he took off, flew around a bit, and landed for the final time. He never flew a plane on his own again.

He cheered on the minor-league Midland Angels, attended backyard barbeques, and played touch football. He didn't forget the civic responsibility lessons that his parents had taught him: he volunteered for the United Way, he taught Sunday school, and he supported the Republican Party, just as they had when they lived in Midland.

After a year in his hometown, he invested a little bit in wells drilled by others. The self-proclaimed "Mr. Frugal" was baffled when the first well was dry. This oil business was not going to be as easy as he had anticipated. He'd invested a few thousand, and then it was gone. But the next well and the next one dribbled some oil, so he made up his loss and added a bit to his bank account.

Happy and content as he seemed, something was missing, and that something was the family business—politics. Of course, he followed his father's political life. When President Gerald Ford appointed George Bush director of the Central Intelligence Agency, he asked George W. to talk to his siblings and find out how they would feel about him taking the job, since the CIA director routinely received criticism for covert actions. George W. wrote him, "I look forward to the opportunities to hold my head high and declare ever so proudly that yes, George Bush, super spook, is my Dad and that yes I am damn glad for my country that he is head of the agency."

EARLY DAYS IN POLITICS

The opportunity to enter politics came when incumbent congressman George Mahon decided not to run for reelection. The 19th District was now wide open, and George W. threw his hat in the ring. His friends told him that money would be no problem and to leave the fund-raising to them. Don Evans volunteered as campaign chair.

With experience gained from his father's campaigns in Texas and the ones in Florida and Alabama, George W. had learned a thing or two about campaigning. He wanted to start early, and he wanted to remain focused on a few critical issues. Midland, Odessa, and Lubbock were the three towns of any size in the district. The first two were oil towns, and George W. expected to do well in those areas. Agricultural interests controlled Lubbock, and he knew little about farm problems, but he told folks he was ready to learn and would represent them well.

In July 1977, George W. announced he would be seeking the congressional seat. This was well over a year before the election. A couple weeks later his plans were sidelined temporarily by a most unexpected event. His friends Joe and Jan O'Neill asked him to a backyard barbeque, and they also invited Jan's former roommate, Laura Welch, who was in Midland visiting her parents.

Appointed by President Gerald Ford (right), George H.W. Bush is sworn in as CIA director in this photo, taken on January 30, 1976. Barbara Bush stands at his side.

Laura grew up in Midland and attended school at Southern Methodist University in Dallas. After graduation, she taught elementary school in Houston and lived in the very same apartment complex where George W. had an apartment while he was in the Guard. However, he lived in the noisy party section, and she lived at the opposite end on the quiet side, so their paths never crossed.

Reading was Laura's passion, and she delighted in reading to her students. This pastime led her to pursue a master's degree in library science from the University of Texas in Austin. For a while, she served as a children's librarian in Houston, then she returned to Austin to work as a librarian in an elementary school. She visited her parents in Midland quite often, and whenever she saw Jan O'Neill, her former roommate would ask if she'd like to meet George W.

Laura knew who he was and vaguely remembered him from his grammar school days in Midland, but each time Jan asked her to meet the bachelor, she declined. She was aware of the Bush legacy, and she wasn't interested in politics. Finally, one summer day, she accepted and re-met her future husband.

The two appeared to be opposite on the outside. As a reporter later wrote, George W., nicknamed the Bombastic Bushkin by his friends, was the type that a librarian would tell to be quiet. But on the inside, the two held very similar values: love of family, respect for others' opinions, and loyalty to friends. After that first evening, Laura told her mother that she liked George W. because he made her laugh. George W. told his parents that he had met a woman who was a great listener, and since he was a great talker, they were a good fit. George W. Bush wrote about Laura in his book *A Charge to Keep*:

> We are not really opposite, although we are different. Laura is naturally reserved; I am outgoing. Laura stays in her own space; I've always invaded other people's spaces, leaning into them, touching, hugging, getting close. Some might mistake her calm for shyness, but they are wrong. She is totally at ease, comfortable and natural, just calm. I, on the other hand, am perpetual motion. I provoke people, confront them in a teasing way. I pick at a problem, drawing it to the surface. She is kinder, much more measured, arriving at a conclusion carefully, yet certainly.

Three months after they met, they married in a simple church ceremony in Midland. They had both served in several big weddings, and they decided they didn't want to plan a huge event with bridesmaids and groomsmen. Neither one had attendants, but they invited their families and closest friends to witness their vows.

Laura made George W. promise that she would not have to give a public speech as his congressional campaign heated up.

But three months later, he told her he had a scheduling conflict and asked her to fill in for him in Muleshoe, Texas. The speech was a test of endurance for her, and she ran out of words.

Laura learned the hard way to take her mother-in-law's advice. Barbara Bush had suggested that she never criticize her husband's speeches. One night when they were pulling into their drive, George W. asked Laura how his speech had gone. When she told him it wasn't very good, he was so dumbfounded, he drove into the garage wall.

GEORGE BUSH FOR CONGRESS

George W. won the Republican nomination over Jim Reese, ex-mayor of Odessa, and set his sights on the general election. His Democratic opponent, Kent Hance, was from the Lubbock area and had the strong backing of agricultural interests. The Hance campaign criticized George W. for being a transplanted easterner because of his Andover, Yale, and Harvard schooling. Hance later bragged that George W. had one of the finest educations available, and he turned it against him. George W.'s first big television ad showed him jogging, which he felt showed him as a man of action. Hance turned that against him, too. West Texans didn't jog for exercise; they worked in the fields.

Although George W. didn't know it, in September a college intern had placed an ad in the Texas Tech student paper announcing a "Bush Bash" with music and free beer. Five days before the November election, a letter from Hance's former law partner was mailed to 4,000 anti-alcohol church members. Staffers wanted George W. to denounce Hance as a hypocrite because he was one owner of land that rented to a nightclub, but George W. didn't want negative campaigning. He later said he regretted that decision. "When someone attacks your integrity, you have to respond."

Much later, a Bush staffer ran into a Democrat who had worked for Hance, who told her that he had written the "Bush Bash" ad and that the college intern had been on the Democrats' payroll. If this is true—and other Democrats say it was a possibility—then it was George W.'s first encounter with dirty politics, though certainly not his last.

On election night, George W. carried the oil areas, but he lost Lubbock and the rural areas. He was disappointed, of course, but he remembered that his father and his grandfather had lost their first elections, too.

With the campaign behind him, George W. poured his energies into his new oil company, Arbusto, Spanish for "bush." His uncle Jonathan Bush helped him set up a limited partnership that would draw investors. With his uncle's Wall Street connections and his own ability as a salesman learned from his land man days, George W. put together a sizeable group of investors and began drilling. Some holes were dry, some held oil, but none were the gushers George W. hoped for. However, managing the company taught George W. that hiring intelligent, capable people and trusting them to do their jobs was the way to instill loyalty in employees. It was a lesson that he kept in the forefront of his mind when he later hired political staffs.

While he worked for Arbusto, he also worked part-time for his father's campaign for president. When George W. spoke on his father's behalf, he strolled confidently to the podium, hit the major points, and sat down. He wore boots that showed he was Western through and through, but he sometimes misjudged his audience. When he was speaking in the East, he was seen as too rough, but in Texas, he was becoming one of the boys.

Ronald Reagan beat George Bush on the road to the Republican convention, but Reagan selected him as his vice presidential running mate, and the subsequent election was an overwhelming Republican victory. With his father as vice president, George W. put his own political ambitions aside. He did not want to run on his father's coattails.

George Bush for Congress

Dear Voters,

Laura and I would like to take this opportunity to thank you for the many kindnesses you've shown us during my campaign for the Congress.

You've listened to me, and you've told me what you think. And hundreds of you have actively worked in my campaign.

I am very grateful to all of you.

During the past twelve months I have told you how much I want to represent you in the Congress. I mean that. I know I can do a good job.

Again, our thanks.

George W. Bush

ON NOVEMBER 7,
VOTE FOR WEST TEXAS.
VOTE FOR
George Bush for Congress

In 1978, with his new bride by his side, George W. Bush ran for Congress. It would be his first experience running for office, but certainly not his last.

By this time, Laura was pregnant with twins, and in the last trimester, she suffered from toxemia. She was hospitalized seven weeks before the due date, but the toxemia worsened, and she delivered twins Barbara and Jenna, named for their grandmothers, five weeks before they were due. George W. was in the room during the cesarean section on

On November 25, 1981, twins Barbara and Jenna Bush were born. The girls are named after their grandmothers and were thrust into the national spotlight during their father's presidential campaign.

November 25, 1981, and he called it the "most thrilling moment of [his] life."

Although his family life was fine, his business was starting a downward slide. The price of oil was dropping, and the jokes around Midland about "Ar-bust-o" provoked George W. enough to change the name of his company to Bush Exploration. The new name couldn't halt the downward price spiral or the dry wells, and in 1984, George W. merged his company with successful Spectrum 7. Part of the deal was stock in the company, and he was retained as chairman.

Now he was back in the business of finding investors, and he again used his family connections and his land man training to strike a deal. Many days he'd leave the house at the crack of dawn, fly out of the Midland airport, and meet with investors that his uncle Jonathan had chosen. But diverse investors couldn't stop the price of oil from sinking even lower. Two years later, Spectrum 7 was in financial trouble, but another buyout, this time by Harken Energy, saved George W. Again he was paid in shares, he was named a director of the company, and he was hired as a consultant for investor relations.

George W. burned the candle at both ends. He worked hard and played hard. As he approached his 40th birthday, he and Laura and some friends planned a getaway weekend in Colorado Springs, Colorado. After a night of heavy drinking, George W. rose early and set out for his morning run, but he had a hangover and his energy was sapped. When he made it back to the hotel, he told Laura that he was through with drinking. And that was that. He didn't make a big deal of it. He continued to go to parties, but he just didn't drink alcohol. He felt more energetic, more focused, and more disciplined than before.

He claimed the seeds were sown for the change a year earlier when he'd had a spiritual reawakening. The Reverend Billy Graham had visited the Bush family at the annual August family reunion in Kennebunkport, Maine. George W. talked at length with the evangelist and returned to Midland to read and study the Bible. His growth as a Christian helped him make the decision to quit drinking.

Some friends claim Laura gave him an ultimatum. She was tired of the drinking and told him to choose between alcohol and her.

His father may have weighed heavily in the decision. George Bush was making a run for the presidency, and George W. didn't want to do anything that would embarrass his father.

Probably a combination of events led him to put down the bottle. As he said, "It is one of the best things I have ever done."

6

The President's Son

TIMING WAS EVERYTHING, GEORGE W. BELIEVED, AND 1988 WAS THE time for his father to run for president. His history studies had shown that few vice presidents were elected president, and George W. wanted to make sure that his father had every chance to succeed.

What Americans perceive as a candidate's image is controlled to a great extent by campaign political advisors. George Bush had selected brash and innovative Lee Atwater to steer his campaign. At a meeting in 1986 at Camp David, the government-owned retreat, the vice president called his family together to meet his team of advisors. George W. and brother Jeb wondered about Atwater's loyalties since his political consulting firm was also courting other presidential candidates as clients.

"How do we know we can trust you?" George W. asked flat out.

"If you're so worried about my loyalty, why don't you come to Washington and help me with the campaign?" Atwater asked. "That way if there's a problem, you'll be there to solve it."

George W. was up to the challenge. He and Laura sold their Midland home in the spring of 1987 and moved the family to Washington. George W. became the loyalty enforcer for the campaign. His father appreciated the devotion and wrote in his diary:

> I think [George] coming up here will be very helpful and I think he will be a good insight to me. He is very level-headed, and so is Jebby. I think some of our political people are thinking, "Oh, God, here come the Bush boys." But, you know where their loyalty is and they both have excellent judgment and they are both spending a bunch of time on this project.

Although he had no official title, George W. had access to the candidate whenever he wanted it. He decided which reporters could have private interviews with his father, appeared at Republican Party fund-raisers, and courted the Christian right, the fundamentalist groups that controlled a large block of voters. Those people who couldn't gain access to the candidate felt if they talked to George W., he would make their opinions known to his father.

He served the same type of role with the campaign staff. He listened to one opinion and then another, sorted through the problem, and reported to his father in a straightforward manner. He learned to listen, he learned to evaluate, and he learned to communicate, all attributes that would be vitally important to him later.

George Bush had not yet declared his candidacy when an unsubstantiated and untrue rumor was started about an alleged affair with a staffer. Atwater's plan was to respond. He leaked the story that George W. had asked his father point-blank and been told no. By quoting George W.'s quip, "The answer to the Big A question is N.O.," to a reporter who printed it, Atwater defused the issue and got the campaign, a campaign that was not yet official, moving forward again. George W., who carefully watched Atwater's skill and resourcefulness, learned how to handle a sticky situation.

In October 1987, George Bush announced he was running for president. The press conference went well, but the accompanying *Newsweek* cover story caused an explosion of anger inside George W. He had given the reporter access to the candidate, even invited her to Kennebunkport to be with the family, and the thanks she showed was in the cover headline, "Fighting the Wimp Factor." George Bush wrote in his diary, "That *Newsweek* story was the cheapest shot I've seen in my political life."

Furious, George W. chewed out the reporter. After all, his father had been the youngest pilot in the navy, had been shot down and rescued, and this reporter had dared to use the word "wimp." The candidate's gentlemanly manners were being held against him. Through the rest of the primary campaign, George W. held reporters at arm's length and was known as the "Roman candle" of the Bush camp. He sparked and exploded when his father was attacked. He became the gatekeeper for reporters to pass through, and he wanted to check their material for accuracy.

He continued to marvel at Lee Atwater's abilities, gaining more respect for and learning all he could from the master strategist. Atwater maintained that a cool persona was critical and that George W. needed to curtail his temper. George W. agreed and worked at calming down his feisty manner.

But again he was livid when, from the podium of the Democratic National Convention broadcast on national television, Texas state treasurer Ann Richards made fun of his father. "Poor George, he was born with a silver foot in his mouth." The often-quoted remark made Barbara Bush physically ill, and George W., never one to take lightly

Vice President George H.W. Bush attends a campaign rally in Omaha, Nebraska, in this 1988 photo. The campaign and Bush's subsequent term in office would prepare his son for the presidency.

any criticism of his father, put Richards at the top of his mental blacklist.

By convention time, George Bush had enough votes to win the Republican nomination. George W.'s siblings announced the vote in their states when the roll call was taken: Neil in Colorado, Jeb in Florida, Dorothy in Maine, and Marvin in Virginia. Although the roll call was in alphabetical order, several states passed so that

George W. could announce the delegate vote in Texas that sealed the nomination. As he cast the 111 Texas delegate votes, George W. said, "For a man we respect and a man we love, for her favorite son and the best father in America . . . the man who made me proud every single day of my life and a man who will make America proud, the next president of the United States."

During the campaign, George W. continued in the role he'd played before the nomination. He kept faithful watch over his father, and he continued to observe Atwater's brand of campaigning, facing every dirty political rumor as if it were a balloon and popping it with a pin.

Before the election, George W. received a call from an old friend from his Spectrum 7 days. The Texas Rangers baseball team was for sale; of course, George W., still an avid baseball fan, was interested. Others across the country were also interested in the team, so George W. quickly resorted to his organizational training as an oil land man and made lists of prospective investors for the big venture.

George W. knew he was going back to Texas after the election. He was still a consultant for Harken Energy, which was headquartered in Dallas, and Texas was home. A few days after his father was elected president, he bought a house in north Dallas. George W. and his family stayed in Washington while he served on the Scrub Team, the committee that decided which people deserved jobs in the White House, but by mid-December, a moving van was taking their belongings back to Texas.

January's Inauguration Day found George W. and family back in Washington watching the parade from the presidential viewing stand. As the University of Texas band marched toward them, George W. put on a ten-gallon hat and grinned a grin as big as Texas.

Campaigning was in his blood, and George W. had never given up the desire to serve in an elected capacity. Now he set his sights on the governorship of Texas in 1990. He ran the idea by a few people and was told this was not his time. He needed a bigger statewide profile, and he needed to do something on his own, like his father had when he left the East and settled in Texas. George W. wasn't convinced 1990 was bad timing for him, and to get a feel for the situation, to get facts on which to base his decision, and to make his name known, he took a swing around the state. He spoke at Lincoln Day festivities and worked for the Republican Party.

THE TEXAS RANGERS

Meanwhile, he was making phone calls about the Texas Rangers. Through his uncle, he had eastern connections just as he'd had in his oil business, but the baseball commissioner wanted more of the purchase price from Texas investors. With help from the commissioner, who convinced a Texas multimillionaire to invest, the deal was completed by the spring of 1989, and George W., who had made the least financial contribution and owned only 1.8% of the team, was named managing general partner and would draw a salary as the public relations man. He believed his campaign experience had taught him how to deal with the media, especially now that he had tamed his temper.

George W. was in seventh heaven; he was actually getting paid to watch baseball. He'd spent his childhood memorizing player statistics; now he mingled with ballplayers at the park, including standout pitcher Nolan Ryan. George W. invited First Lady Barbara Bush to throw out the first pitch in May. She wore a Rangers jacket and posed for pictures with her son. George W. later commented:

> My mother is very good at getting and sending a message to average Americans, and that is because she is just herself. She is funny, she is glib. There's nothing phony about Barbara Bush.

His mother was a huge publicity asset to George W. in Texas. And baseball was an opportunity to become known across the state as a successful businessman, just what his friends had told him he needed before he could run for political office. George W. sat in the stands beside the Rangers dugout in full view of TV cameras instead of sitting high in a relatively hidden owner's box. He had baseball cards made up with his picture to hand out to the crowd, and he autographed them whenever someone asked. He roved the stadium, shaking hands, patting people on the back, and learning the names of the employees, from ticket takers to hotdog vendors.

He still wanted to run for governor in 1990, but Barbara Bush mentioned to a reporter that George W. had better concentrate on baseball for a while. George W. said publicly that his mom was still giving advice out of love and concern for her son. Although off the record he was upset that the decision seemed to be taken out of his hands, he reset his sights on the 1994 race.

Besides, he had plenty of other business on his mind. Harken had been given the lease to drill offshore of Bahrain in the Persian Gulf, and although George W. was not involved in the negotiations, he was the president's son, and his name as a stockholder carried weight. When a big investor approached him to buy Harken stock, George W. saw a chance to sell his shares and pay his baseball team debt owed to a Midland bank. He consulted a Harken lawyer about the ethics of the deal and received the go-ahead to sell.

His sale came shortly before the company announced a second-quarter loss of millions, and his deal drew strong criticism. As a stockholder, he was required to file paperwork with the Securities and Exchange Commission. He filed his intent to sell with the SEC, and he claimed he filed a separate form for an internal sale, but the SEC said they couldn't find it. They said he filed nearly eight months after the filing deadline, and the missing paperwork that was filed on time never surfaced. A short investigation followed, but it was eventually dropped.

Meanwhile, the United States was embroiled in Operation Desert Storm, helping Kuwait drive the Iraqi forces of Saddam Hussein out of their country. George Bush's popularity soared as

Bush talks to reporters at Arlington Stadium on April 18, 1989, after the Texas Rangers were sold to a group in which he was a shareholder. Bush served as managing general partner and public relations manager.

the war was broadcast almost bullet by bullet on television during the short military operation. With the military success of liberating Kuwait from Hussein's forces, it looked like the president would be a shoo-in for reelection, so George W. wouldn't be needed as the loyalty enforcer during the campaign.

George W. was invited to the White House on numerous occasions. He once attended a quiet lunch with his family and Queen Elizabeth II of England. Barbara Bush told the queen that she'd placed George W. far away from her and he was told not to say a word. The queen asked if he was the black sheep of the family, and George W. said he guessed he was. Barbara Bush explained that George W. was dangerous because he said what he felt.

George W. tended to baseball business, and part of it was political. He helped convince the people of Arlington, where the Rangers were based, that a new stadium was absolutely necessary. Once again he was out among the voters, persuading them to believe in him and the project. Voters approved a sales tax increase to pay for the stadium, and in April 1992, George W. drove a front-end loader and tore out a piece of the old parking lot to launch the construction of the new stadium.

During the summer, George W. resigned his position on the board at Harken and devoted his extra time to his father's campaign. Things weren't going well. Third party candidate, billionaire Ross Perot, was courting conservative voters from the president, and Democrat Bill Clinton was climbing higher in the polls.

Master strategist Lee Atwater had died from cancer the year before, and there was no one campaign worker who could focus the campaign as he had done four years earlier. George W. saw that too little was being done too late. Before election day, polls showed that George Bush would not be reelected.

Oddly enough, his father's exit from politics cleared the way for George W.'s political career. Now the timing was right.

7

Governor
Bush

AFTER HIS FATHER'S DEFEAT IN 1992, GEORGE W. KEPT HIS POLITICAL connections with big money Republicans across Texas. But for a man who rarely let his spirits get down, he allowed personal problems to weigh heavily on his shoulders and push his political goals to the back of his mind.

Of course, the presidential defeat bothered him, as did the SEC inquiry into his sold shares of Harken Energy. There was trouble at the ballpark over minority contracts. His brother Neil had been sued by the federal government over a savings and loan that had gone under and was eventually fined $50,000. It seemed that whatever his siblings were doing was reported in the media with a negative spin. His grandmother had died shortly after the election, so his mind was steeped in grief as well as muddled with problems that needed solutions.

Always full of energy, sometimes fidgety, George W. decided to train for a marathon race. Every day he worked at the long distance goal, and in January 1993, he completed the 26-mile Houston Marathon in 3 hours and 45 minutes. He had achieved his goal, and he returned to Dallas a more positive person and focused on where he wanted to go, and that was to the governor's mansion.

Friends from Midland and Austin came to Dallas for closed-door hours-long sessions; they discussed the possibility of unseating Governor Ann Richards, the former state treasurer who on national television had belittled George Bush with her silver foot remark. Ann Richards was quite a character, an outspoken grandmother who liked motorcycles and was popular with Texans.

George W. was confident he could win. Laura was not so sure. She asked him to make certain that he wasn't being pushed into the run by others, but he really wanted to tackle this campaign. She was still not excited about life in the political arena. She had resented the negative attacks made on her father-in-law during his campaign, and even though this was a state election instead of a national one, the press could attack her husband. They could also attack her.

Those who step into politics forfeit their privacy, and Laura feared a tragic event in her past would be resurrected. At seventeen, she was involved in a fatal car accident that claimed the life of a friend. She had been devastated but had worked through the grief and guilt. She did not want to relive that time again.

But by late summer, the decision was made, and George W. began choosing good, loyal people to take on roles in the campaign. He turned to political consultant Karl Rove to mastermind the campaign; he chose Joe Allbaugh of Oklahoma to serve as campaign manager; he convinced Karen Hughes, executive director of the Republican Party of Texas, to resign that job and sign on as his communications director; he hired lawyer Vance McMahan to work on policy by researching the candidate's philosophic ideas and translating them into specific changes to the law.

GEORGE W. WAS A BIT STIFF IN PREPARED SPEECHES, BUT WHEN IT CAME TO WORKING A CROWD, HIS BIG GRIN AND FRIENDLY MANNER TOOK OVER.

Team Bush christened the campaign plane *Accountability One* and decided early that the campaign would be centered on four main issues: tort reform, to do away with multimillion-dollar liability settlements; juvenile crime and how to deal with juvenile offenders; education, giving local governments control over schools; and welfare reform, getting recipients trained for jobs and forcing "deadbeat dads" to pay child support. From years earlier working on the senate campaign of Edward Gurney in Florida, George W. had seen the power of picking a few points and hammering them home over and over. He never lost sight of that during the campaign.

The Bush team decided to hit the rural areas in the first months of 1994, reserving the cities for the fall when the campaign would swing into high gear. By day, George W. shook hands at courthouses, factories, and schools, and in the evenings, he held fund-raisers. He was a bit stiff in prepared speeches, but when it came to working a crowd, his big grin and friendly manner took over. Meeting people one-on-one was his strong suit.

Notably missing from the early months of the campaign were George and Barbara Bush, who didn't want attention detracted from the candidate. But in March, they attended two big fund-raisers for George W. and then flew to Florida to fund-raise for their second son, Jeb, who was running for governor in that state. Each candidate mentioned in speeches, although Jeb said it first, that he was not running because he was George and Barbara's son, but because he was his children's father. They were both looking to the future, not looking back.

George W. reaffirmed that the view was forward, not backward, by refusing to answer a reporter's question on whether he had experimented with drugs, a standard question asked of politicians who came of age in the turbulent 1960s. "What I did as a kid? I don't think it's relevant, nor do I think it's relevant what Ann Richards did as a kid. I just don't think it matters. Did I behave irresponsibly as a kid at times? Sure did. You bet."

George W. pounded on the issues in speech after speech. Governor Ann Richards, always quick with a quip, called her opponent "Shrub," implying that he was the son of a Bush; she called him "Prince George" and "some jerk." She attacked his business history and reiterated the message that he'd never held public office before.

A fall tradition for Texas candidates is a photo-op on opening day of dove season. Even Ann Richards fired a few blanks in the air. But on George W.'s hunt, when his guide shouted, "Dove," the candidate shot and killed the bird as cameras and reporters captured the moment. He proudly picked it up. Unfortunately, he discovered later, the dove was actually a killdeer, a protected species. He immediately called to report it, paid the $130 fine, and at his next news conference told the story and joked, "Thank goodness it was not deer season; I might have shot a cow." The Bush team had thought the public might react negatively, but the killdeer incident became a nonissue because George W. faced it head-on.

Election night found George W., Laura, and the 12-year-old twins headed to a victory celebration in Austin. His 53 percent win over Richards was the biggest margin in a governor's race in 20 years. His brother Jeb didn't win in Florida and called his opponent to concede.

THE WORK BEGINS

The governor's position in Texas government is not the most powerful in the state; the legislature holds more power. Yes,

George W. Bush and George H.W. Bush walk up the South Lawn drive of the White House. Having access to the inner workings of his father's administration helped prepare George W. for his own campaign and presidency.

Republican George W. had a bully pulpit to make his views known and steer his agenda, and he had veto power over legislation, requiring a two-thirds vote to override. He also appointed the secretary of state, the parole board, and commissioners of various agencies, which controlled management of the state, but Democrats led the legislature. Leading the Senate was Lieutenant Governor Bob Bullock—a Democrat; the Speaker of the House was Democrat Pete Laney.

George W. Bush called on both men and told them he wanted to work with them for the good of Texas. He arranged weekly breakfast meetings with them, and he began courting members of the state legislature with his main theme of doing what was right for Texas. He excelled at the backroom meetings, one-on-one with legislators. He appointed Clay Johnson, his former college roommate, to recommend appointments to the various boards and commissions. He told Johnson to find the best people for the jobs and not let party politics enter into choices. A product of the good-ol'-boy system, George W. appointed some qualified people who had helped elect him, people who were loyal to him, people he could trust.

The Texas legislature meets only 140 days in two years. When it was in session, George W. wheeled and dealed to make his campaign promises realities. And although legislation was passed on all four of his campaign issues, the bills did not go as far as he had hoped. Plans were made to return control of education to local boards; several welfare cuts were passed; stricter penalties were set for juvenile offenders; and a bill was passed to reduce monetary rewards for frivolous lawsuits.

When the legislature wasn't in session, time weighed heavily on George W's hands. A *Texas Monthly* article lined out his working day as starting at the office at 8:00. He'd leave around 11:40 for a jog and lunch, and then return around 1:30. If there were no meetings, he stayed in his office to be available, but he played video golf or solitaire until 3:00. Evenings ended early. Official dinners were over by 9:00.

Appointments were brief. At the end of the allotted meeting time, an aide would knock on the door to end the meeting. If he needed more time, George W. would wave the aide away, but he'd expect a second knock five minutes later. George W. relied on his staff to thoroughly research issues and present them to him in a summary, not a lengthy policy report. He'd read the summaries and then hone in on crucial elements. He'd assign an aide an opposing view so that he had both sides of an issue. Then he'd analyze both sides, reduce the issue to its core, and make a decision.

Trusting the consensus opinions of his commissions, George W. usually reinforced their decisions. Most decisions were not headline makers, but two very different cases claimed the public's opinion. In both cases, the governor followed the same criteria in seconding the Texas Board of Pardons and Paroles' opinion, which was: "Is there any doubt about the guilt of the individual, and has the individual had a fair hearing and full access to the courts?"

The first case dealt with pickax murderer Karla Faye Tucker. In prison, she became a born-again Christian, and the evangelical community, along with celebrities and anti-capital punishment groups, asked that George W. step in and grant her a 30-day delay, all that a Texas governor is allowed for a death-row inmate, so she could seek further legal action, even though in this case there was no doubt that she was guilty. She did not pass George W.'s two-question test for clemency, so he allowed the execution of the first woman in Texas since the Civil War.

The second case involved Henry Lee Lucas, a self-proclaimed serial killer. He was convicted of killing a woman, identified as "Orange Socks" for the only clothing she was wearing when her body was found. Lucas confessed to that killing and hundreds of others, but later he recanted the Orange Socks murder. Proof emerged after the trial that he was in Florida when the killing occurred. The prison board advised the governor to stop the execution. Again, George W. applied

The first woman executed in Texas since the Civil War, convicted murderer Karla Faye Tucker was denied clemency by George W. Bush, governor of the state. In prison, Tucker became a born-again Christian and even married the prison chaplain. Although many religious and political leaders believed Tucker had reformed and should not be put to death, Bush showed no mercy.

his two-question test. Lucas is the only death-row inmate whose execution was stopped, and in court, he was sentenced to life in prison, with no possibility of parole.

His capital punishment decisions were brought up by George W.'s opponent, Garry Mauro, in the 1998 campaign for governor, but another issue received more press. Was George W. biding time in Texas awaiting a run for the country's top job? In Republican meetings, his name had surfaced many times as not only a contender for president but as a front-runner.

George W.'s standard reply to the questions was, "I don't know whether I'll seek the presidency or not." He stuck to Texas politics during the campaign and earned the backing of many Democrats in the legislature, including Senate leader Bob Bullock. It was no surprise when George W. Bush won with an impressive 67 percent of the vote, the first time a Texas governor had been elected to successive terms.

Still, reporters asked the question again and again. Some reports surfaced that a possible presidential bid looming in the distance prompted the partners in the Rangers to sell the team. George W. received around $15 million for his share. The deal made his decision easier. Now he was free to pursue a higher office without regard to his financial future if he weren't elected.

The morning of his second inauguration as governor, George W. listened to the minister speak at a special service. Pastor Mark Craig said that people are "starved for leadership, starved for leaders who have ethical and moral courage." People wanted leaders who would do what was right.

"He was talking to you," Barbara Bush later told her eldest son.

George W. thought so, too, and set his sights on Washington.

8

The Presidential Election

BEFORE "REALITY DAY" FOR THE ELECTIONS OF 1998, THE ELDER GEORGE Bush wrote a letter to George W. and to Jeb, who was once again running for governor of Florida. He told them not to worry about what reporters wrote even though it could be hurtful to their family:

> At some point both of you may want to say "Well, I don't agree with my Dad on that point" or "Frankly I think Dad was wrong on that." Do it. Chart your own course, not just on the issues but on defining yourselves. No one will ever question your love of family—your devotion to your parents.

The two brothers won the elections in their respective states, and for George W., the road that led to Washington was filled with the pitfalls of comparisons that his father had foreseen. The two shared the same name, except that George W. was missing the Herbert in his father's name, and the son strikingly resembled his father. Not since John Adams and John Quincy Adams had a son followed his father to the presidency, so the possibility of it happening again caused a media frenzy.

With the decision to run made, George W. knew he had some serious homework. He had little knowledge of foreign affairs, and as was his custom, he surrounded himself with intelligent foreign policy experts, many of whom had worked for his father's administration, and listened to their different views on the United States' relations with various countries. He also needed to define his own key issues, much as he had when he ran for governor.

In meetings with advisors, he asked questions like an outsider, like a consultant brought in to change a company's outdated policies to workable policies. Instead of fixing a system, such as health care, he asked experts how they would establish a health care system from scratch. He tackled military weapons the same way. If there were no tanks used in the military, would weapons experts suggest some be built? On the economy, he asked how to spur growth and settled on cutting taxes to let people spend more of their own money.

With his policy statements in place, Bush still knew the presidential race would be character-based. President Bill Clinton's dalliance with a White House intern and later impeachment, but not conviction, on charges of obstruction of justice and perjury before a grand jury in a civil case, made voters think of who they wanted to lead the country in terms of trust. But before George W. could face the Clinton-tainted Democratic nominee, most likely Vice President Al Gore (although he was challenged briefly by former senator Bill Bradley), George W. had to win the Republican nomination.

The field of Republican candidates widened as more and more candidates joined the campaign trail. By September 1999, several candidates had dropped out, but eight remained. George W. was the front-runner, but Arizona senator John McCain was closing in. Others in the field included Gary Bauer, an ultraconservative who had worked in the Reagan White House; Elizabeth Dole, former secretary of transportation and former secretary of labor; Steve Forbes, wealthy publishing giant; Orrin Hatch, senator from Utah; Alan Keyes, who had previously worked at the United Nations and the state department, but had never held elective office; and Dan Quayle, former vice president under George Bush.

In his campaigns for governor, George W. had not brought up his family connections, but in the presidential campaign, he did not discourage questions about his parents. When one reporter asked why he was the front-runner, he quipped, "Maybe it's because I have a famous mother." Name recognition, critical to candidates, was not a problem for him.

"His personality and temperament come from Barbara," said his wife, Laura. "They both love to needle and they both love to talk." Bush even wisecracked that he had his father's eyes and his mother's mouth, not a bad comment considering that Barbara Bush is one of America's most admired first ladies.

George W. had become an impressive campaigner. *Texas Monthly* writer Paul Burka noted his style when he followed the governor during a 1998 campaign trip, a style George W. continued during the presidential bid.

> He works a crowd the old fashioned way, going through it rather than waiting for the people to come to him. He makes eye contact and holds it; I followed him around the room in Eastland [Texas] and I never once saw his eyes stray from a voter to survey the room. Bush is a toucher: he doesn't shake a hand so much as grab it; he leans in close, clutches an arm, pats a shoulder, gives a hug. "Hey, buddy," he'll say, or "'Preciate your takin' the time."

The governor's campaign style got even better as he moved toward the primaries in 2000, but once again, questions of his youthful behavior surfaced. Responding to reporters' questions on purported drug use, he answered maybe he did or maybe he didn't. Just as he'd said in his earlier campaigns, he maintained that questions about past behavior were not relevant to the election.

He said, "When I was young and irresponsible, I was young and irresponsible," and he refused to elaborate. He wanted the election to be about the issues and who a person was as an adult.

Although John McCain posed a serious threat in the first of the primaries, by Super Tuesday in March, when fourteen states elected delegates to the Republican National Convention, George W. was all but guaranteed the nomination. Through the remaining primaries, he campaigned not just against other Republicans but also aimed his words at Al Gore, who had virtually won the Democratic nomination when the votes were counted on Super Tuesday. The vice president had been in national politics for more than two decades. George W. was a newcomer on the national level. Instead of downplaying the difference, he played up the outsider role, claiming he would bring fresh ideas to Washington.

At the Republican National Convention, George W. Bush was selected as the party's candidate. George W. asked Dick Cheney to be his vice presidential running mate. Cheney had the national government experience that George W. lacked. Cheney had served as White House chief of staff for President Gerald Ford, had been elected six times as congressman from Wyoming, and had served as secretary of defense in George Bush's administration.

At the Democratic National Convention, Al Gore picked Joe Lieberman, senator from Connecticut, as his running mate. Other candidates represented small political parties, most notably environmentalist Ralph Nader, running for president for the Green Party, and ultraconservative Pat Buchanan, the presidential candidate for the Reform Party.

After the conventions and until Election Day on November 7, the candidates campaigned fast and furious. George W.'s campaign, under the direction of Midland friend Don Evans, set records for fund-raising. The Republicans were ready to stand

Republican presidential candidate Texas Governor George W. Bush, right, and Democratic presidential candidate Vice President Al Gore debate on October 3, 2000, at the University of Massachusetts at Boston.

behind a man who said he was a compassionate conservative who could serve both the right-wing conservatives of the party and the more moderate Republicans. The campaign chest held more than $90 million, and George W. refused matching funds from the government that came with strings attached. His campaign could spend campaign money without government regulations.

To campaign crowds, George W. came across as friendlier than Al Gore, who seemed stiff and formal. On national TV and radio, George W. faced Al Gore in three debates. Both sides claimed victories, although Al Gore earned criticism for his loud sighs, interrupting, and arrogant behavior. "Arrogant" had been a word applied to George W. during his youth, but he had learned to stay calm, cool, and conveyed a confident air at the debates. Viewer polls showed that the debates did not change the mind of voters who had already settled on one candidate.

On the Thursday before the Tuesday election, reports circulated that 24 years earlier Bush had been convicted of driving while under the influence of alcohol. Bush admitted that was true, but he said he had changed. Team Bush hoped the news would not influence the evangelical right to vote against him, but memory of the university beer bash ad during that long ago congressional election in Texas flashed back.

ELECTION CONTROVERSY

On November 7, the presidential race was too close to call. Polls by both parties showed that some states would go strongly for Al Gore and others would easily elect George W. Bush, but there were a handful of states in which the candidates were evenly matched. In each state, the candidates were competing for the popular vote, which would dictate which way the electors in the electoral college would cast their votes.

Instead of electing the president and vice president by popular vote, each state has electors, the same number as the state has U.S. congressmen (decided by the state's population) and senators (two). Of the 538 electoral votes, a candidate needed 270 to win the presidency. The electoral college was included in the Constitution to balance large and small states. If it did not exist, states with large populations, such as New York, Texas, and California, could control an election, and the election would not be a true national contest.

Both candidates settled in for the long wait. With the election so close, it could be long into the night before a president was elected. In Austin, George W. gathered his friends and family around him. Jeb was with him that evening, as were the forty-first president and Barbara Bush.

The Bush family was dining at a restaurant when television newscasters called Florida for Al Gore. Florida was a critical state, with 25 electoral votes. Jeb didn't believe the call was accurate; he was convinced that George W. would win that state. The family retreated to the privacy of the governor's mansion where they could view the results without reporters around. At that moment, the election seemed to be going Gore's way.

The Voter News Service (VNS), headquartered that night in the World Trade Center, is jointly owned by television networks (CBS, ABC, NBC, FOX, CNN) and the Associated Press. On Election Day, thousands of temporary employees stood outside voting places and conducted exit polls. They recorded age, race, gender, religion, income, past voting tendencies, and for whom a person voted. This information was sent to computer banks at VNS that plugged the numbers into statistical models and forecasted the winner of each state. In many states, a winner could have been announced by early afternoon, but by agreement, networks waited until polls closed in a state before predicting the winner. But on November 7, newscasters prematurely called Florida before the polls closed in the panhandle. They had forgotten that part of the state is in the central time zone.

Jeb Bush phoned campaign workers in Florida and discovered that something wasn't right. The samplings VNS based their call on were skewed toward Gore. The Bush camp was cheered by the news, but the networks stood by their call. Team Bush was concerned that the declaration, which made it look like Gore would win the presidency, could influence voters not to vote for a losing cause in other states, where polls were open for two more hours.

Quickly, two other key states, Pennsylvania and Michigan, were tallied in the Gore column, and the Bush camp was somber until the central border states (Missouri; Tennessee, Al Gore's home state; Arkansas, Clinton's home state) were called for Bush. It was not until shortly after 10:00 P.M. that the networks recalled their Florida decision and placed it in the too-close-to-call category. A couple hours later, with the reported electoral count at 246 for Bush and 255 for Gore, it was clear that those 25 electoral votes in Florida would determine the presidency. Around two in the morning, Florida was put in the Bush column based on a 50,000-vote lead, and the networks named George W. Bush the next president. Al Gore called George W. and conceded. Gore left his hotel suite to deliver his concession speech at his headquarters. Before he reached the podium, his advisors learned that the margin in Florida was a mistake, a computer glitch, and only several hundred votes separated the two candidates, which meant an automatic machine recount of votes, mandated by Florida state law. Gore called George W. and retracted his concession, saying that Florida was still too close to call.

By daylight Wednesday, George W. Bush led the tally by less than 2,000 votes. A machine recount began immediately. Lawyers from both sides flew into Florida. On Thursday, the Gore team asked for hand recounts in four heavily Democratic counties. In every election in every state, votes are not counted because of voter error, but the percentage was unusually high in some Florida counties. In Florida, punch-type ballots were used, and if a chad, a rectangle that was to be punched out, wasn't fully disconnected, the machine would not count it. These were "undervotes," and the Democrats wanted every one counted where the voter's intent could be determined.

By Friday, the machine recount was completed. Gore trailed by barely 300 votes (without absentee ballots counted), and his team insisted that the undervotes be counted. A few precincts using punch-type ballots were counted on a trial basis, but the standard of perceiving voter intent was controversial and subjective. If a chad hung by two sides, was it a vote? Or if the chad was punctured, but didn't dislodge any sides, was that a vote? What about a "dimpled" chad? Perhaps the voter meant to vote but didn't push hard enough with the stylus. The Gore camp would benefit if every dimpled chad were counted. The Bush camp protested.

The Democrats also cried foul over a butterfly ballot used in one county that listed the ten slates of president/vice president candidates from large and small political parties on both sides of the ballot with the voting holes in the middle. This ballot confused some voters, who voted for more than one candidate for president.

Many lawsuits were filed in both state and federal courts asking to hand count the ballots, stop the hand count, extend the deadline for counting, stay the extension, challenge the overseas ballots, and challenge the standard of counting. Late evening on December 12, in a 5 to 4 decision, the U.S. Supreme Court decided that the deadline would not allow a hand recount that had no fair and uniform standard. Many Democrats felt they had been cheated out of a victory; many Republicans felt the election was finally legitimate.

On December 13, Al Gore gave a gracious concession speech on national television. He said it was time to put partisan rancor aside. Although he disagreed with the Supreme Court ruling, he said he accepted it. "Tonight," he said, "for the sake of our unity of the people and the strength of our democracy, I offer my concession."

George W. Bush gave his victory speech in the chamber of the Texas House of Representatives. He mentioned that he understood how difficult this was for the vice president and then moved on to speak in reconciliatory terms.

> I was not elected to serve one party, but to serve one nation. The president of the United States is the president of every single American, of every race and every background. Whether you voted for me or not, I will do my best to serve your interests, and I will work to earn your respect.

The controversial election with Supreme Court intervention caused concern and dismay across America. After George W. Bush was declared the winner, several news organizations began independent examinations of the undervote and

Protests in front of the U.S. Supreme Court reveal the strong emotions stirred up by the 2000 presidential election. The court decided in *Bush v. Gore* to end hand recounts of the ballots in Florida, granting George W. Bush the presidency.

overvote. In June 2001, *USA Today* and several other newspapers declared Bush had won the election by using three of four standards of evaluating undervote ballots. However, if the overvote was counted, those ballots that had more than one vote for president, Gore's name was punched in combination with others more often than Bush's. It would be impossible to discern voter intent from these ballots. Some people had voted for all ten candidates.

One thing was clear. Election equipment and voter education needed to be addressed, not only in Florida but across the nation.

9

Attack on the Nation

ON JANUARY 20, 2001, GEORGE WALKER BUSH WAS INAUGURATED AS the forty-third president. Instead of immediately focusing on him, media followed the news story of former president Bill Clinton because of his questionable eleventh-hour pardons of many people. Without a great deal of media hype, President Bush settled into Washington life surrounded by people he trusted for their loyalty to him and their expertise in their fields. His appointees to the cabinet were made and confirmed by the Senate.

The president started his workday in the Oval Office by 6:50, earlier than he did when he was governor. But his job was much more complex than his job as governor because of foreign policy. He said:

Because of our standing in the world, the United States is expected to be active everywhere in the world: right now

George W. Bush takes the oath of office from U.S. Supreme Court Chief Justice William Rehnquist to become the forty-third president on Saturday, January 20, 2001, in Washington, D.C.

in Macedonia, Ireland, Korea, the Middle East, Iraq. The irony is that Europe is anxious for our help, yet at the same time, they want to tie our hands; they are trying to bind us to international treaties that restrict our capacity to act, and I'm not going to let them do that.

In February, U.S. submarine *Greeneville* surfaced in a routine drill and hit a Japanese fishing boat, killing nine people on board and injuring others. The situation called for delicate handling, and President Bush informed the Japanese that he "regretted" the incident and promised an investigation.

The world received disturbing news from Afghanistan in March. The Taliban, the radical fundamental Muslim rulers of that country, declared that two huge Buddha statues, both between 1,600 and 1,800 years old, were blasphemous and must be destroyed. Although other nations, including the United States, viewed the statues as masterpieces to be treasured, the Taliban blew them up with explosives.

In April, a Chinese plane collided midair with an American spy plane, which made an emergency landing on a Chinese island. The Chinese demanded an apology, and they would not release either the 24-member crew or the plane. Days later, the president again used the word "regret" to show remorse on the part of the Americans for violating Chinese airspace. The men were returned and the plane was shipped in pieces back to the United States. It appeared that U.S-Chinese relations were not harmed because of this situation.

In May, national affairs demanded the attention of the Bush White House. The FBI discovered it had not turned over some 3,000 documents to the defense team of terrorist Timothy McVeigh, convicted of the 1995 bombing of the federal building in Oklahoma City that killed 168 people. The Justice Department delayed McVeigh's scheduled May 16 execution until attorneys could determine if the additional documents could have changed the defense. The outcome only delayed McVeigh's execution until June 11, but questions were raised about the death penalty, which President Bush had dealt with head-on when he was governor of Texas.

In New York City, two Muslim extremists were convicted of the 1998 bombings of United States embassies in Kenya and Tanzania in which 224 people were killed. The two were linked to the international terrorist organization al Qaeda, lead by Osama bin Laden, who adamantly did not want American presence in the Holy Land. Among the documents entered into testimony was a training manual that directed terrorists to blend into the country where they were sent. They were instructed to discard their native Arab robes and wear fashionable clothes and behave like those in the country they had infiltrated. But the terrorist threat was seen to be overseas, in Europe and Africa.

In June, President Bush rejected the Kyoto Protocol, which called on nations to reduce emissions of carbon dioxide and other greenhouse gases in an effort to combat climate change. He believed it went against economic growth, and he doubted the scientific basis for the United Nations' sponsored international treaty.

In August, President Bush announced his decision on federal funds used for stem cell research. A scientific advance showed that embryonic stem cells could regenerate tissue for many parts of the body. Antiabortion groups opposed the use of embryonic stem cells, calling them part of a human being, even though many of the stem cells were from in-vitro storage and would be thrown away. President Bush presented a compromise. He allowed federal funds for research on the 64 lines already in development, but he disallowed funding for new lines.

SEPTEMBER 11, 2001

The day that changed the nation began like a normal day on the road for President Bush. He was in Sarasota, Florida, to speak at an elementary school about reading and education.

He rose before daybreak, slipped on khaki shorts, a large white T-shirt, socks, and running shoes and was off for a jog. He wanted to get the kinks out, release energy, and start his day right.

Reporters followed the president on his run, and by the time he was walking in his cool-down phase, the sun had peeked over the horizon. A reporter asked how many miles he'd run, and the president replied, "Four and a half."

Bush returned to his hotel, received his routine national security briefing, and arrived at Emma E. Booker Elementary School eager to speak about education. Before he was introduced to a class of second graders, he was taken to a holding room and informed that a plane had hit the north tower of the World Trade Center in New York City. A myriad of possibilities raced through his mind. Surely it had been an accident, a plane with mechanical failure or a pilot trying to ditch the plane in the harbor and missing.

Bush, looking worried, left the holding room and was introduced to the second graders. He was listening to them read when chief of staff Andrew Card walked into the room and whispered in the president's right ear that another plane had flown into the second tower. The president's head reeled to the left, as if he'd been hit. He bit his lip, and his gaze darted from the students to the floor to the teacher, his distracted thoughts not on reading but on what had to be a terrorist attack on the United States. For nearly six minutes, he sat in the classroom so he wouldn't alarm the children, his mind racing to responses to the attacks. As he rose to his feet to walk out, a reporter asked him if he was aware that a plane had crashed in New York.

He held up his hand as if to stop the words. "We'll talk about it later," he said and strode to the holding room where he was updated on the horrific events. He immediately placed phone calls while watching TV pictures of the two burning towers.

Around 9:30, over a half-hour late for his scheduled speech, he was ushered into a large room where 200 local officials, school administrators, teachers, and students waited. Instead of his prepared speech, a solemn president explained that others would be discussing education in his place and he would be returning to Washington. In a stiff manner he read:

> Today we've had a national tragedy. Two airplanes have crashed into the World Trade Center in an apparent terrorist attack on our country.

Chief of Staff Andrew Card informs President George W. Bush about the attacks on the World Trade Center on September 11, 2001. Bush had been visiting the Emma E. Booker Elementary School in Sarasota, Florida, when he received the stunning news.

I have spoken to the Vice President, to the Governor of New York, to the Director of the FBI, and have ordered that the full resources of the federal government go to help the victims and their families, and to conduct a full-scale investigation to hunt down and to find those folks who committed this act.

Terrorism against our nation will not stand.

As President Bush was taken to the Sarasota airport, where bomb-sniffing dogs had thoroughly searched Air Force One, he learned that the terrorist attack wasn't over. Another hijacked plane had hit the west side of the Pentagon. Within minutes, the White House was evacuated after authorities determined it could be the destination of a fourth hijacked plane.

Forced by Federal Bureau of Investigation agents to a bomb-proof shelter in the basement of the White House, Vice President Dick Cheney picked up a secure phone and called the president. He strongly urged him not to return to Washington at that time. FBI and other law enforcement agencies believed that not only the White House but also the president's plane was a target.

Air Force One took off from Florida with a secret destination and with a fighter escort. It flew at a high altitude and changed directions several times. In his office on the plane, Bush watched on TV as the Twin Towers collapsed and spoke on the phone to his wife and to his advisors. He was overheard saying, "That's what we're paid for, boys. We're gonna take care of this. We're going to find out who did this. They're not going to like me as President."

Already the Federal Aviation Agency had shut down all U.S. airports, and air traffic controllers were scrambling to land all airborne planes, some 4,400 flights, at the nearest airports. Bush had made the decision for the military to shoot down any other hijacked planes if they approached populated areas. Bridges into Manhattan were closed. Wall Street had halted trading. Warships were taking up positions off the East Coast. Across America, citizens were watching TV in shock, numb with disbelief.

Bush wanted to speak to the nation before his plane reached its ultimate destination, Offutt Air Force Base in Nebraska, the most secure military post in the country. By now the president knew that a fourth hijacked plane had crashed in a Pennsylvania field instead of its planned target, which FBI surmised to be the White House or the Capitol.

Bush's plane scheduled a stop at Barksdale Air Force Base near Shreveport, Louisiana. Two fighter jets, one on each wing,

"THE RESOLVE OF OUR GREAT
NATION IS BEING TESTED. BUT MAKE
NO MISTAKE: WE WILL SHOW
THE WORLD THAT WE WILL
PASS THIS TEST."

–George W. Bush

escorted the plane to the airstrip. Only when local reporters discovered that Air Force One had landed did the rest of the country know the whereabouts of the president.

Bush was ushered by military guards in full combat gear to a building where he delivered a message to TV cameras. "Freedom itself was attacked this morning by a faceless coward. And freedom will be defended . . . The United States will hunt down and punish those responsible for these cowardly acts." Reading from a script, a stern-faced Bush informed Americans that U.S. military at home and abroad was on high alert status and that security precautions were in place to insure the functions of the government. "The resolve of our great nation is being tested. But make no mistake: We will show the world that we will pass this test."

Once again, Bush climbed the steps to board Air Force One, and this time he was flown to Nebraska. Here he was secured in an underground bunker where he held a teleconference with the National Security Council. He started the meeting with a forceful policy statement. "We are at war against terror, and from this day forward, this is the new priority of our administration."

Meanwhile at FBI headquarters in Washington, Bush's trusted counselor Karen Hughes spoke to the press on his orders, assuring Americans that the president had directed that the federal emergency response plan be implemented. The Secret Service had secured members of the national security team, the cabinet, and senior staff members in various locations. The government was operating. Banks were open. The

Department of Health and Human Services had sent personnel and supplies to the attack scenes.

Against Secret Service adamant warnings, around 4:30 P.M., President Bush headed back to Air Force One, telling reporters he wasn't going to let terrorists keep him out of Washington. He arrived in Washington around 7:00 and addressed the nation from the Oval Office at 8:30. He talked about the victims of the attack.

> These acts of mass murder were intended to frighten our nation into chaos and retreat. But they have failed; our country is strong.
>
> A great people has been moved to defend a great nation. Terrorist attacks can shake the foundations of our biggest buildings, but they cannot touch the foundation of America. These acts shattered steel, but they cannot dent the steel of American resolve.
>
> America was targeted for attack because we're the brightest beacon for freedom and opportunity in the world. And no one will keep that light from shining.

President Bush assured the nation that the evacuations of government buildings on this day were for security reasons but that they would be open for business the next day. He thanked world leaders who had called with condolences and offers of help. In one sentence, he summed up how he was going to deal with terrorists. "We will make no distinction between the terrorists who committed these acts and those who harbor them."

After the speech, he gathered his primary national security advisors in the White House bunker for a meeting. By now it was known that the terrorists were members of an extremist Islamic group known as al Qaeda. How would the war on terrorism be fought?

Central Intelligence Agency director George Tenet, who had been appointed by Clinton and retained by the new president because he thought the man was trustworthy and intelligent, said that al Qaeda was headquartered in Afghanistan. But it operated worldwide in 60 countries.

"Let's pick them off one at a time," President Bush said.

Every avenue open to the federal government was suggested to fight the terrorists: military, financial, diplomatic, and covert operations by the CIA. A coalition of countries united to fight terrorism would be built.

On Wednesday, September 12, the nation was still in shock. Bush made stronger statements, saying the attacks were more than acts of terror—they were acts of war.

Bush was criticized by some for not being in the public eye for six hours while he was in the secure bunker in Nebraska. Government spokesmen again reiterated that Air Force One was a suspected target. Indeed, on Wednesday morning an airplane, which on Tuesday had taken off from New Jersey and flown its routine route to Florida, was swarming with FBI agents, who suspected this plane would have been a fifth hijacked plane had terrorists' plans not somehow gone awry.

Late afternoon on Wednesday, Bush and Secretary of Defense Donald Rumsfeld visited the Pentagon. Bush addressed the workers and said he felt both sad and angry, but his remarks seemed planned, not spontaneous and sincere.

Thursday morning Bush paced behind his desk in the Oval Office while talking on the phone to New York City mayor Rudy Giuliani and New York governor George Pataki. It was a photo opportunity with cameras on the two men in New York and on the president in Washington. Bush's words were awkward and sounded unnatural; a replay of words spoken earlier about a new kind of war. His delivery sounded like a poorly rehearsed speech.

After he hung up the phone, he took a few questions from reporters. He justified not returning immediately to Washington as an appropriate action for a commander in chief and then took a question about his prayers during this time. He said he was thinking about the victims. Blinking back tears, he said, "I am a loving guy, and I am also someone, however, who has got a job to do, and I intend to do it. This country will not relent until we have saved ourselves and others from the terrible tragedy that came upon America." This was the leader Americans had been waiting to see—a man shaken by emotions but resolved to make good decisions that would see the country through the disaster and the days of his promised war against terrorism.

When Bush met with the two senators from New York, Hillary Rodham Clinton and Charles Schumer, offering aid for their state, they asked for $20 billion. He didn't hesitate and immediately agreed that it was appropriate help for New York City. He also commented on the financial cost of the war that he knew would take time to plan.

"When I take action, I'm not going to fire a $2 million missile at a $10 empty tent and hit a camel in the butt. It's going to be decisive."

On Friday, President Bush spoke at Washington National Cathedral at the National Day of Prayer and Remembrance for those lost in the attacks. Seated beside him and First Lady Laura Bush were his parents, former president George H.W. Bush and Barbara Bush. Former presidents Bill Clinton, Jimmy Carter, and Gerald Ford and their wives sat in the congregation. Bush had also invited former vice president Al Gore, whom he had defeated for the high office less than a year earlier in a tight and highly contested election. Solidarity was in the faces of these officials; they were all Americans first and partisan politicians second as they listened to Bush's eloquent words.

> War has been waged against us by stealth and deceit and murder. This nation is peaceful, but fierce when stirred to anger. This conflict was begun on the timing and terms of others. It will end in a way, and at an hour, of our choosing.
>
> In every generation, the world has produced enemies of human freedom. They have attacked America, because we

are freedom's home and defender. And the commitment of our fathers is now the calling of our time.

When President Bush took his seat, his father reached out and patted his arm in a gesture of respect and approval, a gesture that reflected the feelings of a nation. The younger man shook his father's hand.

That afternoon President Bush flew to New York City and was stunned by the sight at Ground Zero, the site where the Twin Towers had stood. Smoke still rose from the many fires in the debris as he walked among the ruins.

He had not planned to speak, but the exhausted workers wanted to hear from him. He climbed atop a burned out fire truck and someone handed him a bullhorn. In a loud voice, he told somber rescue workers that the nation mourned with them. Someone yelled, "I can't hear you." He yelled back, "I can hear you." The crowd erupted in cheers and laughter, a first since that awful Tuesday. The president repeated, "I can hear you. The rest of the world hears you." Again he was interrupted with applause. "And the people who knocked these buildings down will hear all of us soon." The crowd chanted, "U.S.A! U.S.A!" The president had connected with the workers and rallied them when they were in great need of an emotional lift.

That night in Washington, Congress granted Bush the power to make war, and the plans to wage the war against terrorism continued to take shape in meetings at the Pentagon and meetings with the National Security Council.

CHAPTER

10

The War on Terror

PRESIDENT BUSH GATHERED HIS CAREFULLY CHOSEN ADVISORS AROUND him on the morning of September 15 at Camp David, the presidential retreat in Maryland. He listened to CIA director Tenet outline his plan for a war against the al Qaeda terrorist training camps headed by Osama bin Laden in Afghanistan: use both CIA and military commandos to aid Afghanistan's Northern Alliance, the anti-Taliban force, while airplanes drop bombs on terrorist camps and Taliban strongholds. General Hugh Shelton, chairman of the joint chiefs of staff, presented military options.

Afghanistan was a nation of 26 million and about the size of Texas, but it was undeveloped with few roads. Although the Taliban headed the national government, different tribes controlled local areas with tribal chiefs in command. These so-called warlords could be bought with enough money, but they might also play one side against the other.

Following the September 11 attacks, President Bush met with his cabinet and advisers at Camp David. From left sit Attorney General John Ashcroft, Vice President Dick Cheney, President Bush, Secretary of State Colin Powell, Secretary of Defense Donald Rumsfeld, and Deputy Secretary of Defense Paul Wolfowitz, FBI Director Robert Mueller, Secretary of the Treasury Paul O'Neill, CIA Director George J. Tenet, White House Chief of Staff Andy Card, National Security Adviser Condoleezza Rice, and Chairman of the Joint Chiefs of Staff Gen. Henry H. Shelton.

The advisors discussed that the war had to be global in scope to rout out terrorists. Iraq and Iran were on a list of countries that supported terrorists, and Iraq's leader, Saddam Hussein, was viewed as a man who would not hesitate to sell weapons of mass destruction to terrorists. Secretary of State Colin Powell said a coalition of Muslim nations supporting the U.S. war would crumble if the war were waged outside of Afghanistan and not just against al Qaeda. Defense Secretary Rumsfeld was of the opinion that the coalition would have to change depending on the targeted country.

President Bush voiced his belief, "At some point we may be the only ones left. That's okay with me. We are America."

Shortly after lunch, Bush told his team of advisers to get some rest or exercise and report back at 4:00. At that meeting, he asked for individual recommendations. All wanted military action, but there were different ideas on what type of action was appropriate. He thanked them all and told them he needed time to think about it.

By the next afternoon at the White House, Bush had made a decision. He wanted the war marketed as a fight against terrorism, which threatened all nations, instead of merely an American retaliation. The campaign would start in Afghanistan with both CIA and military operatives, both in the air and on the ground.

Bush told Americans that this war would not be like other wars, and he identified as a prime suspect Osama bin Laden, who organized terrorist training camps in Afghanistan and whose work had been supported by the Taliban regime, the rulers of that country. The terrain of that desolate land would demand a different type of warfare.

Bush also reminded Americans that it was time to go back to work, to get the country moving forward, and to fight terrorism by not letting it intimidate America. To underscore this message, on Monday, September 17, he went to the Executive Office Building next to the White House and met office workers as they arrived for work.

That afternoon he spoke briefly at the Islamic Center in Washington. Because the terrorists had been identified with the extremist Muslim terrorist group al Qaeda, across the nation there had been isolated negative reactions against Arabs and followers of the Islamic religion. Bush's remarks were aimed at making a distinction between the terrorists and Muslims. "The face of terror is not the true faith of Islam. Islam is peace," he said.

Bush needed a bigger stage to deliver his message that the war wasn't against Arabs but against a specific segment, and that stage was at the Capitol in front of a joint session of Congress.

On September 20, Bush welcomed British prime minister Tony Blair to the White House. Blair represented America's best ally in the war against terror. He sat in the audience and watched Bush stride into the Capitol and give the speech of his life. Some 82 million Americans watched on television, at homes, in bars, and even at a hockey game in Philadelphia, where fans demanded the game be stopped and the speech be on the stadium's video screens. Bush held the attention of millions more around the world. Newspapers printed the full text of his eloquent message the next day.

In his speech, Bush demanded that the Taliban in Afghanistan turn over bin Laden or they would share in the fate of that terrorist. He spoke to nations around the world, saying they had a decision to make: either they were with the United States or they were with the terrorists. And he told Americans:

> Great harm has been done to us. We have suffered great loss. And in our grief and anger we have found our mission and our moment. Freedom and fear are at war. The advance of human freedom—the great achievement of our time, and the great hope of every time—now depends on us. Our nation—this generation—will lift a dark threat of violence from our people and our future. We will rally the world to this cause by our efforts, by our courage. We will not tire, we will not falter, and we will not fail.

The leader of this generation was facing the challenge. George W. Bush believed he had found his mission and his moment.

President Bush met with Pakistani president Pervez Musharraf to discuss a military operations base in Pakistan to launch an attack on the al Qaeda camps in Afghanistan. The president left the details to his staff, as was his custom. He decided broad policy and expected his staff to implement his decisions. In this case, he credited Secretary of State Powell as single-handedly getting Musharraf to cooperate with the United States.

The first troops on Afghan soil, just 16 days after the attack, were CIA paramilitary, who prepared the way for ground troops and coordinated with the Afghan Northern Alliance. On October 7, President Bush addressed the American people on national television from the Treaty Room in the White House, announcing he had ordered air strikes to commence in Afghanistan in an operation called Enduring Freedom. To show the Afghan people that the war was against terrorists and not them, he also announced the dropping of food and medical supplies.

> We are joined in this operation by our staunch friend, Great Britain. Other close friends, including Canada, Australia, Germany and France, have pledged forces as the operation unfolds. More than forty countries in the Middle East, Africa, Europe and across Asia have granted air transit or landing rights. Many more have shared intelligence. We are supported by the collective will of the world.

The war would require patience and sacrifice. He warned Americans that the war would not be without risk of life, and he thanked the men and women of the military who would be fighting the war on foreign soil. "Your mission is defined; your objectives are clear; your goal is just. You have my full confidence, and you will have every tool you need to carry out your duty."

When a few weeks later the campaign seemed stalled and the press emphasized that the war was bogging down, President Bush did not lose faith. At a meeting with his advisors, he stopped their voiced concerns about the war. "We did all agree on the plan, didn't we?" They agreed. "I've made it clear to the American people. I've got confidence in this plan. We should all have confidence in this plan. Be patient, people. It's going to work."

A few days later, the Taliban retreated from several cities, and the fall of the zealots looked imminent. President Bush was

Plumes of smoke rise from the Taliban-controlled village of Rahesh, north of Afghanistan's capital Kabul on November 9, 2001. Days of punishing U.S. air strikes helped the Northern Alliance break through outer Taliban defenses. In 10 days, the Taliban lost two-thirds of its territory and saw its government fall into the hands of its greatest enemies.

pleased, but he knew the war against worldwide terrorism was not over. And bin Laden's location was unknown.

At home, another element of terrorism further threatened previously complacent Americans. A deadly bacterium, anthrax, had been sent in letters to a television newscaster and to a senator and a congressman. Post offices were examined carefully. A government office building was shut down while it was sanitized. Security measures were put into effect for those handling mail. Tom Ridge, director of the newly created agency Homeland Security, handled the security details, while FBI agents followed every lead in an effort to find the person responsible for several anthrax deaths.

Stopping another terrorist attack on American soil topped Bush's agenda. Forty-five days after September 11, Congress passed the Uniting and Strengthening America by Providing Appropriate Tools Required to Intercept and Obstruct Terrorism Act, known by the acronym USA PATRIOT Act. This bill expanded the government's right to wiretap telephone calls, search homes and computers, access medical records, deport immigrants, and arrest and hold enemy combatants. The government issued a no-fly list to keep suspected terrorists or associates from flying commercial airlines.

The economy, which had been falling, continued a slide into a recession despite interest rate cuts. In order to promote the economy, President Bush traveled through the Midwest. He followed the route of products from the time they were manufactured to their export and advocated increasing the selling of agricultural products abroad.

The soldiers in Afghanistan were fighting a unique brand of war. In the rough mountainous landscape riddled with caves, horses were more useful than tanks, and television news showed pictures of U.S. soldiers on horseback in contrast to sophisticated U.S. air strikes against known airfields. As they routed out the Taliban forces and al Qaeda members, soldiers searched many convoys headed for the border, but many enemy forces slipped into Pakistan.

On December 7, 2001, the Taliban's southern stronghold in Afghanistan fell, leaving the country in the hands of the United States and the Afghans against the Taliban. There was no official peace treaty signing, but there was a shift in power. With

United Nations support, an Afghan leader was selected to head an interim government before a constitution and elections could be held to set up a permanent government.

In his January 2002 State of the Union address, the president reminded Americans that the war in Afghanistan would not be over until that nation had a stable government. The hunt for terrorists in other countries would continue through a combined effort of nations.

He called Iraq, Iran, and North Korea an "axis of evil" because they were developing weapons of mass destruction. His words gave Americans a hint of war on another front:

> I will not wait on events, while dangers gather. I will not stand by, as peril draws closer and closer. The United States of America will not permit the world's most dangerous regimes to threaten us with the world's most destructive weapons.

Terrorism in the Middle East now focused on the Israeli-Palestinian conflict, which had festered once again. Palestinian suicide missions escalated. President Bush saw the Palestinian Authority chairman Yasser Arafat as a terrorist. Indeed, a younger Arafat had led the anti-Jewish group, Fatah, and Bush believed Arafat had the power to call off the suicide and terrorist attacks claimed by the Hezbollah and Hamas terrorist groups, but instead Arafat did not interfere. Bush had earlier said, "A lot of this violence is provoked by Arafat's inactivity; we've got to send a very strong signal that the terror must stop…"

When Bush had spoken to the United Nations, he refused to meet Arafat. The Palestinian made his way toward Bush for a handshake, but Colin Powell intervened and hustled the president out before an awkward moment of refusal.

Bush called on the Palestinians to "elect new leaders, leaders not compromised by terror." He believed Israeli's prime minister Ariel Sharon needed to be realistic about the conflict, withdraw his people from Palestinian areas, and allow a Palestinian government to form a recognized country.

Bush wanted peace between Israel and Palestine and in the Middle East, and he believed a democratic Iraq would be a step toward it. In 1991, during the presidency of George H.W. Bush, the United States defended Kuwait when dictator Saddam Hussein's troops had invaded that small country. In the short Gulf War, American troops pushed Iraq's forces back into their own country, but they did not pursue them past the border. Northern Iraq and southern Iraq no-fly zones were maintained by American military aircraft. When U.S. pilots were shot at, they fired back, but no planes had been downed.

INVADING IRAQ

Toppling the regime of the dictator was not the mission of the Gulf War, but now President George W. Bush believed the time was right to invade the country, depose Hussein, and install a democratic government. An Arab democracy in the Middle East would send a signal to other Arab countries. It would also be a needed base and ally in finding terrorists in other countries.

Why invade Iraq? President Bush presented the case that Hussein had used chemical weapons of mass destruction against his own countrymen, the Kurds, in the northern part of Iraq. Would a leader who hated Americans be reluctant to share these weapons with al Qaeda terrorists? President Bush believed it was only a matter of time until Hussein put even bigger weapons, nuclear weapons, in the hands of terrorists. He saw the war on Iraq as a preemptive war, striking at an enemy before it could strike the United States. Hussein was compared to Adolf Hitler, the German leader who led the Axis powers in World War II. If democracies had not appeased Hitler but instead stopped him before he took over so many European countries, history would have been quite different. Now Bush wondered what Hussein would be like in five years if he remained unchecked.

The United Nations had sent inspectors into Iraq after the Gulf War to make sure no nuclear, chemical, or biological weapons of mass destruction were being made. But in 1998, Hussein kicked the inspectors out.

President Bush met with British prime minister Tony Blair at Camp David and discussed the problem of the rogue state. Blair said he agreed on action with the United States, even war, but felt the U.N. should be consulted. On September 12, 2002, Bush went to the U.N. and asked for resolutions to act against the threat of Hussein. But by early October, the U.N. had not yet agreed on its resolutions.

The delay by the U.N. did not deter the president. He wanted the backing of Congress on Iraq before the mid-October adjournment. On September 26, he told some congressional members, "If we use force, it will be fierce and swift and fast." The next week, at a meeting with members of the House International Relations Committee, he called Hussein a liar. "He is playing the international community for a fool.... Australia, Slovakia, Czech Republic, England—these countries are all on our side."

Weapons of mass destruction were suspected, but concrete numbers were lacking. Still, President Bush in a speech on October 7 said, "Facing clear evidence of peril, we cannot wait for the final proof—the smoking gun—that could come in the form of a mushroom cloud."

On October 10, the House authorized the president to use U.S. armed forces in Iraq "as he deems to be necessary and appropriate." The Senate passed the resolution the next day.

In November, the U.N. Security Council passed a resolution telling Hussein that if he didn't disarm as he'd promised years earlier, he would face serious consequences. Weapons inspections began again, and nothing was found. Yet intelligence information showed substances were being moved before inspectors began their jobs. Foreign journalists were taken to chemical facilities and shown only one area, not the entire complex. They were told the factory was producing insecticides, not poisons for people.

At the same time America purported to hold out for diplomacy, war plans were being drawn. If the United States was going to war, then it had to be no later than March because of the brutal weather in Iraq. There was no doubt in the president's mind that the military would be successful, but he met with Iraqis living in America to find out how Iraq would react to democracy. He heard that they would make it work and that the United States' presence would be required for two or three years after Hussein was ousted.

Although European community members, particularly France and Germany, were reluctant to join a military alliance with the United States against Iraq, by mid-January President Bush had decided that war was the only way to get rid of Hussein. The decision weighed heavy on him as he thought of the Americans who would lose their lives and others who would be injured.

He visited with veterans of the Afghanistan war at Walter Reed Hospital. He awarded a Bronze Star to a seriously wounded sergeant, who could barely speak. The sergeant said he'd like to stand up for the president, but President Bush said, "No, you don't. I'm standing up for you."

Bush said he did not visit the hospital to remind himself of what lay ahead with another war; of course he knew there would be military casualties. He found comforting widows and orphaned children a difficult task, but it was one that the leader of the country should do.

President Bush chose Secretary of State Colin Powell to deliver another call for action against Iraq to the United Nations. He wanted the blessing of the U.N., but he was prepared to act without it. The Security Council stewed for weeks, but when it was crystal clear that France would veto the new resolution against Iraq, it was pulled from the floor on March 17.

That night, President Bush addressed the nation via television from the White House. "All the decades of deceit and cruelty have now reached an end. Saddam Hussein and his sons

In downtown Baghdad, a statue of Saddam Hussein topples on April 9, 2003. This scene was broadcast on televisions around the world and was viewed as a symbol of victory.

must leave Iraq within 48 hours. Their refusal to do so will result in military conflict, commenced at a time of our choosing."

The war began on March 19. That morning, Bush talked with the commanders in the Middle East via secure video link from the Situation Room in the White House. "For the peace of the world and the benefit and freedom of the Iraqi people, I hereby give the order to execute Operation Iraqi Freedom. May God bless the troops." During the day he was updated on the stealth movements of troops. He learned the Polish special forces team had gone into the country. Australians had moved into the west. By evening, spies had learned of Hussein's location, and as soon as bombs were dropped on that area, the president went on television to announce the early stages of the war had begun.

By April 9, Baghdad had been taken. A statue of Saddam Hussein was pulled down on live television and replayed often on the news. The northern part of Iraq was still in enemy hands, but many divisions of Hussein's army had been beaten.

Although President Bush had said there should not be victory dances in the war on terror because there were many fronts to the long war, he celebrated. He wore a green flight suit, sat in the cockpit of a jet, and landed on the aircraft carrier USS *Abraham Lincoln* off the coast of California. In front of a massive banner that read, "Mission Accomplished," he declared that major combat operations in Iraq were over but that there was much work ahead. He linked the war to terror and peace in the Middle East:

> We are committed to freedom in Afghanistan, Iraq and in a peaceful Palestine.
>
> The advance of freedom is the surest strategy to undermine the appeal of terror in the world. Where freedom takes hold, hatred gives way to hope.

Indeed, the fighting continued as resistance forces resorted to guerrilla warfare, suicide bombs, and attacks on the new Iraqi government, new Iraqi police force, and American troops.

The ongoing violence in Iraq became an issue that divided the country and antiwar demonstrations continued as the president made his Thanksgiving Day secret trip to Iraq.

Two and a half weeks later, U.S. troops found Saddam Hussein hiding in a narrow underground hole. Although he was in custody, the fighting was far from over.

CHAPTER

11

A Second Term

THE GROUND FORCES IN IRAQ SUFFERED MANY MORE CASUALTIES AFTER THE major offensive was declared over than they had before. And still there were no weapons of mass destruction found. The news reported some parts of a gas centrifuge used to enrich uranium buried in the yard of an Iraqi scientist, and there were known amounts of U.N. banned substances never accounted for, but there were no stockpiles found, and President Bush's image suffered. One of his selling points on the war was the likelihood that Hussein would give the weapons to terrorists to use against the United States.

If there were no weapons, many Americans claimed there was no reason for the war in Iraq. This would be a rallying point against the reelection of the president.

Karl Rove, President Bush's political consultant in his first presidential race, began a grass roots movement to reelect the president as soon as the inauguration was over. This time he planned on a clear victory in Florida with no necessary recount to remind the nation of the hanging chads of the previous election.

President Bush had no rival for the Republican nomination and said he would keep Vice President Dick Cheney on the ticket. Both watched with interest as a field of 10 Democrats vied for the nod to represent their party. At first, it appeared to be a close race, and the front-runner changed as candidates entered the field and primaries were held. But by mid-March 2004, long before the Democratic convention was held in July, it was clear that Massachusetts senator John Kerry would be the presidential nominee. He picked North Carolina senator John Edwards as his vice presidential running mate.

The campaign heated up as the candidates squared off. Oddly, there were similarities between Senator Kerry and President Bush. Both were graduates of Yale, and both were members of the secret society Skull and Bones. But although they were both educated at a private school, they viewed the world quite differently. President Bush viewed his opponent as a pseudo-intellectual who flip-flopped on the issues. Senator Kerry saw President Bush as a sarcastic in-crowd kind of guy who didn't know much.

The campaign dealt with the issues of the war in Iraq, health care, social security, abortion, homeland security, and gay rights. Although the issues would have been plenty to focus on, the campaign got personal, because people end up voting for the person they like the most or sometimes dislike the least.

The 2004 campaigns topped the billion dollar mark, a first, but that number was not just money spent by the candidates. Some television ads were funded by independent advocacy groups, which did not funnel money into the political parties. One such group was the Swift Boat Veterans for Truth.

President George W. Bush delivers a speech to supporters in Tampa, Florida, on October 31, 2004.

A huge personal issue between the two candidates was military service. President Bush was in the National Guard, but he never served in Vietnam. Senator Kerry served in the navy during the war in Vietnam and earned three Purple Hearts (a Purple Heart is an award given to those injured or given posthumously to those killed in action against an enemy). Several veterans who had served in swift boats alongside Kerry attacked his service record and said one of the Purple Hearts was undeserved. They also attacked him for returning to the United States to protest the war and calling the men who served with him "war criminals." Kerry said the ads were lies, although he had, at age 27, testified in front of the Senate Foreign Relations Committee to protest the war.

President Bush was attacked on television's *Sixty Minutes II* for not serving his time in the National Guard. Host Dan Rather claimed to have long-lost documents proving that Bush shirked his duty. Charges that the documents were forged, which they were later proven to be, took the focus off the president and his time away from the Guard and refocused the issue on media bias and reporting.

By the time of the first presidential debate, the Bush–Cheney ticket was ahead in the polls. After the first debate, Kerry gained percentage points. The president had grimaced over and over while listening to Kerry's words. The split television screen showed his reactions, which didn't go over well with media pundits who called the debate for Kerry.

By the second debate, President Bush had been well coached by campaign directors and kept a mild demeanor. Republicans thought he had won the debate, but the Democrats felt they had won it. In the third debate, Kerry referred to Vice President Cheney's openly gay daughter as a lesbian, and the focus groups monitored during the debate had a negative reaction to his words, which were seen not as an innocent remark but as an attack.

Protesters speak out against the nomination of Judge John Roberts as the new associate justice on the U.S. Supreme Court. Roberts's conservative views, particularly his views on abortion, were a source of controversy for many Americans.

Both political parties had tremendous get-out-the-vote campaigns with thousands of new voters registered each day as the campaign raced toward Tuesday, November 2. On Election Day, large numbers of voters stood in line. Exit polls showed a tight race, with the Republican ticket falling behind. By early afternoon, it was apparent that the exit polls were flawed. That evening, as Florida fell into the Republican column, President Bush breathed a sigh of relief. There would be no replay of the 2000 election chaos. The crucial state of Ohio was not called for the incumbents until the early morning hours of Wednesday.

John Kerry made an eloquent concession speech. He spoke about "the danger of division and the need, the desperate need, for unity, for common ground, for coming together." President Bush also touched on the theme of unity in his victory speech.

Two days after the election, President Bush stood before the press corps answering questions. He sounded the tone for his second term. "I earned capital in the campaign, political capital, and I intend to spend it. It is my style." Without another election to campaign for, he felt free to pursue his agenda of Social Security reforms, the war against terror wherever it might lead, and continued tax cuts.

Shortly after the election, Palestinian leader Yasser Arafat died. President Bush did not mourn his passing but saw it as an opportunity for a new Palestinian leader to emerge to pursue a peaceful settlement between Palestine and Israel. More than 1,000 Israelis had died at the hands of terrorists since 2000, but the peace process and resettlement were moving forward with Israelis vacating the Gaza Strip. In an attempt to combat Palestinian terrorism, yet still help rebuild the area, the U.S. policy became not to extend any financial aid to projects, such as streets or schools, if they were named after terrorists who were killed.

On the domestic front, President Bush chose two Supreme Court justices to fill the vacancies left by the death of Chief Justice William Rehnquist and the retirement of Justice Sandra Day O'Connor. New chief justice John Roberts took his seat when the court began its October 2005 schedule. Justice Samuel Alito took her seat in January 2006.

President Bush pushed the federal government to solve problems of slow response to deadly Hurricanes Katrina and Rita in the Gulf coast states. Because neglected levies in the New Orleans region collapsed, parts of the city were flooded. President Bush vowed to help Louisiana and local officials rebuild the city.

President Bush had been elected during peacetime, but events thrust him into global leadership as the world took on

President Bush tours an area of New Orleans damaged by Hurricane Katrina on September 2, 2005. The president was criticized for his administration's delayed response to the disaster.

international terrorism. He sent troops to Afghanistan and Iraq, and as of 2006 they are still fighting in those areas.

He believed that the job was his calling and his leadership qualities were equal to the tasks ahead. He said, "I will seize the opportunity to achieve big goals. There is nothing bigger than to achieve world peace."

CHRONOLOGY

1946 George Walker Bush is born on July 6 in New Haven, Connecticut.

1948 Moves with family to Texas.

1961 Enters Phillips Academy in Andover, Massachusetts.

1964 Works as a campaign aide for his father's Senate race; enters Yale University.

1968 Graduates from Yale; joins Texas Air National Guard.

1975 Graduates from Harvard Business School; moves to Midland, Texas, to work in the oil industry.

1977 Decides to run for U.S. Congress; meets Laura Welch in the summer and marries her on November 5; forms Arbusto oil company.

1978 Wins Republican primary for congressman in June; loses general election in November.

1981 George W. Bush's father becomes vice president of the United States; Laura gives birth to twin daughters, Jenna Welch Bush and Barbara Pierce Bush, on November 25.

1984 Merges his oil company with Spectrum 7.

1986 Sells Spectrum 7 to Harken Energy, which retains him as a director.

1987 Moves to Washington, D.C., to help with his father's presidential campaign.

1988 His father is elected president of the United States; at the end of the year, George W. moves his family to Dallas.

1989 Helps put together a group of investors to buy the Texas Rangers baseball team; becomes managing general partner and deals with the public and press.

1990 Sells Harken Energy stock to pay off his debt for Texas Rangers.

1994 Runs for governor and defeats incumbent Ann Richards.

1998 Sells interest in Texas Rangers; wins a second consecutive term as governor.

1999 Enters presidential race.

2000 Wins contested presidential race against Al Gore.

2001 Inaugurated as the forty-third president of the United States; declares war on terrorism after September 11 attacks; declares war on Afghanistan's Taliban and al Qaeda.

2003 Declares war on Iraq; visits troops in Iraq.

2004 Wins reelection as president against John Kerry.

2005 Inaugurated for a second term; faces domestic emergencies caused by hurricanes Katrina and Rita; nominates chief justice of the Supreme Court.

2006 Makes surprise visit to Iraq to meet with new democratically elected government officials.

BIBLIOGRAPHY

Alterman, Eric, and Mark Green. *The Book on Bush: How George W. (Mis)leads America*. New York: Viking, 2004.

Bush, Barbara. *A Memoir*. New York: Charles Scribner's Sons, 1994.

Bush, George. *All the Best: My Life in Letters and Other Writings*. New York: Scribner, 1999.

Bush, George, with Victor Gold. *Looking Forward: An Autobiography*. Garden City, N.Y.: Doubleday, 1987.

Bush, George W. *A Charge to Keep: My Journey to the White House*. New York: HarperCollins, 1999.

Dershowitz, Alan M. *Supreme Injustice: How the High Court Hijacked Election 2000*. New York: Oxford University Press, 2001.

Engel, Richard. *A Fist in the Hornet's Nest: On the Ground in Baghdad Before, During & After the War*. New York: Hyperion, 2004.

Felix, Antonia. *Laura: America's First Lady, First Mother*. Avon, MA: Adams Media, 2002.

Fleischer, Ari. *Taking Heat: The President, the Press, and My Years in the White House*. New York: William Morrow, 2005.

Goldstein, Joshua S. *The Real Price of War: How You Pay for the War on Terror*. New York: New York University Press, 2004.

Gormley, Beatrice. *President George W. Bush: Our Forty-third President*. New York: Aladdin Paperbacks, 2001.

Greene, John Robert. *The Presidency of George Bush*. Lawrence, KS: University Press of Kansas, 2000.

Greenfield, Jeff. *"Oh, Waiter! One Order of Crow!"* New York: G.P. Putnam's Sons, 2001.

Hersh, Seymour M. *Chain of Command: The Road from 9/11 to Abu Ghraib*. New York: HarperCollins, 2004.

Hughes, Karen. *Ten Minutes from Normal*. New York: Viking Penguin, 2004.

Ivins, Molly, and Lou Dubose. *Shrub: The Short but Happy Political Life of George W. Bush*. New York: Random House, 2000.

Lewis, Charles, and the Center for Public Integrity. *The Buying of the President, 2000*. New York: Avon, 2000.

McGeough, Paul. *Manhattan to Baghdad: Dispatches from the Frontline in the War on Terrorism*. Crows Nest, NSW, Australia: Allen & Unwin, 2003.

Minutaglio, Bill. *First Son: George W. Bush and the Bush Family Dynasty*. New York: Random House, 1999.

Mitchell, Elizabeth. *W: Revenge of the Bush Dynasty*. New York: Hyperion, 2000.

Political Staff of the *Washington Post*. *Deadlock: The Inside Story of America's Closest Election*. New York: Public Affairs, 2001.

Radcliffe, Donnie. *Simply Barbara Bush: A Portrait of America's Candid First Lady*. New York: Warner, 1989.

Thomas, Evan, and the Staff of *Newsweek*. *Election 2004: How Bush Won and What You Can Expect in the Future*. New York: Public Affairs, 2004.

Wukovits, John F. *George W. Bush*. San Diego: Lucent, 2000.

Woodward, Bob. *Bush at War*. New York: Simon & Schuster,

Woodward, Bob. *Plan of Attack*. New York: Simon & Schuster, 2004.

FURTHER READING

Andersen, Christopher. *George and Laura: Portrait of an American Marriage.* New York: William Morrow, 2002.

Braude, Joseph. *The New Iraq: Rebuilding the Country for Its People, the Middle East, and the World.* New York: Basic Books, 2003.

Bruni, Frank. *Ambling into History: The Unlikely Odyssey of George W. Bush.* New York: HarperCollins, 2002.

Clark, Richard A. *Against All Enemies: Inside America's War on Terror.* New York: Free Press, 2004.

Frum, David. *The Right Man: The Surprise Presidency of George W. Bush.* New York: Random House, 2003.

Ivins, Molly, and Lou Dubose. *Bushwhacked: Life in George W. Bush's America.* New York: Random House, 2003.

Moore, James, and Wayne Slater. *Bush's Brain: How Karl Rove Made George W. Bush Presidential.* Hoboken, N.J.: John Wiley & Sons, 2003.

PHOTO CREDITS

INDEX

About the Authors

VEDA BOYD JONES enjoys the challenge of writing for diverse readers. She is the author of 39 books, including fiction and nonfiction for both adults and children, and over 300 articles and stories for magazines and reference books. Jones earned a master's degree in history at the University of Arkansas; has taught writing at Crowder College in Neosho, Missouri; and teaches for the Institute of Children's Literature. She is a past president of the Missouri Writers' Guild. She and her husband, Jimmie, an architect, have three sons. Contact her through her Web site: www.vedaboydjones.com

ARTHUR M. SCHLESINGER, JR. is the leading American historian of our time. He won the Pulitzer Prize for his books *The Age of Jackson* (1945) and *A Thousand Days* (1965), which also won the National Book Award. Professor Schlesinger is the Albert Schweitzer Professor of the Humanities at the City University of New York and has been involved in several other Chelsea House projects, including the series *Revolutionary War Leaders*, *Colonial Leaders*, and *Your Government*.